CONTENTS

Starboard quarter of USS *Texas*. (Judi Burr)

Library of Congress Cataloging-in-Publication Data

Names: Burr, Lawrence, author.
Title: Battleship Texas : Lawrence Burr.
Description: Annapolis, MD : Naval Institute Press, [2023] | Series: Naval
   history special edition
Identifiers: LCCN 2022048288 | ISBN 9781591149095 (paperback)
Subjects: LCSH: Texas (Battleship : BB-35)--History. | BISAC: HISTORY /
   Wars & Conflicts / World War II / General | HISTORY / Military /
   Vehicles / Land
Classification: LCC VA65.T44 B87 2023 | DDC
   623.825/20973--dc23/eng/20221007
LC record available at https://lccn.loc.gov/2022048288

INTRODUCTION

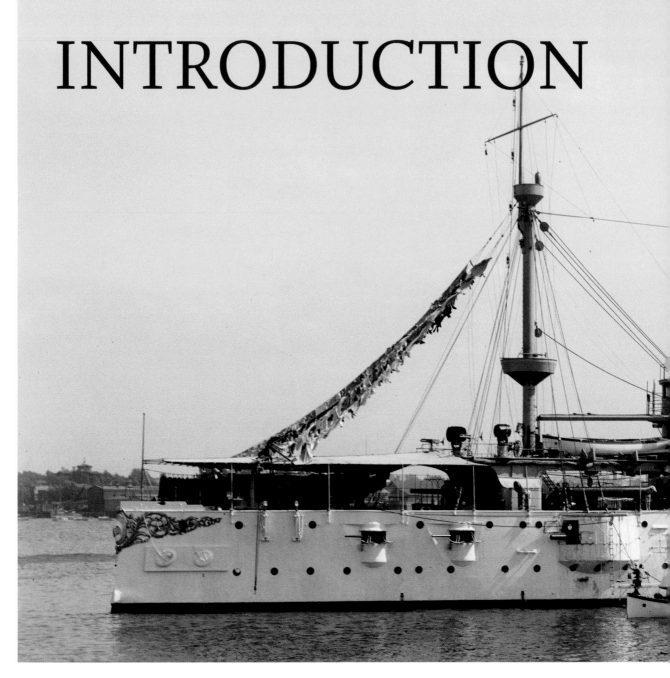

On 21 April 1948, a tired, hard-worked, storm and battle-damaged warship from the 1914–18 dreadnought era was saluted in a bayou off the Houston Ship Canal, adjacent to the San Jacinto Battleground State Park. This park marks where General Sam Houston defeated the Mexican army and secured independence for the state of Texas from Mexico.

Fleet Admiral Chester Nimitz, a Texan, who had recently retired as the Chief of Naval Operations after having been Commander-in-Chief Pacific Ocean Areas, together with Assistant Secretary of the Navy Mark Andrews, were present at the ceremony. Their responsibility was to present the ship to the state of Texas. Captain Charles Baker, the last commanding officer of USS *Texas*, would formally decommission her as a ship of the U.S. Navy.

USS *Texas* (BB-35) had originally been commissioned on 12 March 1914, had been on active service with the U.S. Navy for over thirty-two years, and had served through two world wars. Too old and no longer needed by the Navy, she needed a new mission if she was to be saved from the ship-breakers' yard to become scrap metal.

By the end of the decommissioning service, this ship was "Battleship *Texas*," with a new mission: to act "as a permanent memorial for the purpose of commemorating

The first U.S. Navy battleship, USS *Texas*, at anchor in Boston for the centennial celebration for USS *Constitution*, October 1897. (Library of Congress)

the heroic participation of the State of Texas in the prosecution and victory of the Second World War."

But Battleship *Texas* was and is much more than a memorial—she is a piece of living history of that period when the United States emerged and then solidified its position as the world's greatest economic and military power.

USS *TEXAS*

USS *Texas* is the second warship in the U.S. Navy to bear the name of the state of Texas. USS *Texas* was authorized by Congress on 24 June 1910, launched on 18 May 1912, and commissioned on 12 March 1914, as the thirty-fifth battleship of the U.S. Navy. This date marked the beginning of thirty-two years of operational service.

If 21 April 1948 marked the end of USS *Texas'* commission as a U.S. Navy ship, it commenced her life as a doorway back into a transformative era of American history in which she was an active participant in two world wars, carrying thousands of American sailors safely to the wars' successful conclusions.

HISTORICAL PERSPECTIVE

When commissioned, USS *Texas*—at 27,000 tons normal load, carrying ten 14-inch guns in five turrets, heavily armored, and capable of 21 knots—was the most powerful dreadnought in the world's navies. She also marked a milestone in the development of the U.S. Navy. Her real origins are found in 1883, when Secretary of the Navy William Chandler obtained congressional approval to build four new warships from steel. These ships—known as the "ABCD ships," *Atlanta*, *Boston*, *Chicago*, and *Dolphin*—provided the impetus for American companies to invest in and establish the industrial shipbuilding capability required for the development of a steel navy. From the end of the Civil War until 1883, the U.S. Navy had given up its war-driven technological leadership, reverting to wooden hulls and sails for its warships, with the exception of several monitors for coastal defense.

Both the Crimean War (1853–56) and the U.S. Civil War (1861–65) had shown that the use of iron in ship construction provided a measure of protection from, initially, cannon balls and later exploding shells. This sparked a major developmental race in new warship design and construction, its results exemplified by *La Gloire* in France and HMS *Warrior* in Great Britain in the 1860s. The ongoing development of battleships in the 1870s saw the emergence of battleships of the French *Formidable* and *Courbet* classes and the British *Collingwood* class in the 1880s. This period of naval construction saw the introduction of steel alloy, harder than iron, and the development of steel-based armor in ships. Of particular relevance to the United States were *Riachuelo* and *Aquidaba* of Brazil and *Esmeralda* of Chile. These ships, all designed and built in 1883 by Great Britain, were far more powerful than any U.S. Navy ship and would have easily defeated them in combat. Agitated commentary in American newspapers claimed that these ships could dominate the main seaports and population centers of both the East and West Coasts of America in the event of war between the United States and either Brazil or Chile.

In August 1886, Congress authorized the construction of an armored cruiser, USS *Maine*, and the first U.S. Navy battleship, USS *Texas*, a predreadnought, as latter known—it would displace 6,417 long tons, carry two 12-inch guns in two single-gun turrets, and steam at just under 18 knots. Reflecting the nation's lack of experience in shipbuilding and producing armor plate, *Texas* took six years to complete. She was commissioned in August 1895. (See the appendix for the career of this earlier *Texas*.)

By 1907, the emerging industrial and technological might of the United States allowed the U.S. Navy to build and send sixteen predreadnought battleships as

USS *Texas* en route from the Dry Tortugas to Galveston, February 1898. (Library of Congress)

a combined "Great White Fleet" to circumnavigate the world, a feat no other navy had accomplished. In August 1519, Magellan's five-ship fleet had sailed from Seville and attempted to sail around the world, but only the carrack *Victoria,* under Captain Elcano, survived to return to Seville, in September 1522.

By 1907, the impact of the Spanish-American War and its two naval battles of Manila Bay and Santiago had had a dramatic effect on America's military and diplomatic might. America had expanded its territorial reach to include the Philippines, Guam, the Hawaiian Islands, Puerto Rico, and Guantanamo Bay. As important, President Theodore Roosevelt had stared down Kaiser Wilhelm II of Germany over Venezuela and thwarted Germany's strategic push to undermine the Monroe Doctrine and gain influence and bases in South America. Roosevelt had achieved this diplomatic success by concentrating in the Caribbean the U.S. Atlantic Fleet, under the command of Admiral of the Navy George Dewey, the victor of the battle of Manila Bay, and threatening to go to war.

The period between the authorization of *Maine* and *Texas* and the sailing of the Great White Fleet was one of strong debate and extensive analysis within the U.S. Navy. The rapid expansion of the Navy and the lack of interface between its seven bureaus—Navigation, Ordnance, Equipment, Construction and Repair, Steam Engineering, Supplies and Accounts, and Medicine and Surgery—had led to increasing criticism by serving officers of the system of naval administration and of the ships that were built by this system. An article in *McClure's Magazine,* January 1908, by Henry Reuterdahl detailed the more serious problems. Reuterdahl had not served in the U.S. Navy, but as the American editor of *Jane's Fighting Ships* (published in London), the world's premier authority on the world's navies, he was very influential.

Reuterdahl's main criticisms of U.S. battleships were that their main waterline armor belts were underwater when the ship was fully loaded; that the forward decks up to the gun turret were too low relative to the waterline, risking flooding of the gun turret; that the main gun turrets each had an open shaft from the turret

house to the magazine; and that the gun ports were too large, vulnerable to incoming shells. Reuterdahl saved his main criticism, however, for the Navy's bureau system and its ineffectiveness in addressing and solving the major problems of existing battleship designs.

These design flaws came to a head, to some extent, at a conference at the U.S. Naval War College, at Newport, Rhode Island, in the summer of 1908. Chaired by President Roosevelt, the conference reviewed the defeat of the Russian navy by the Japanese fleet led

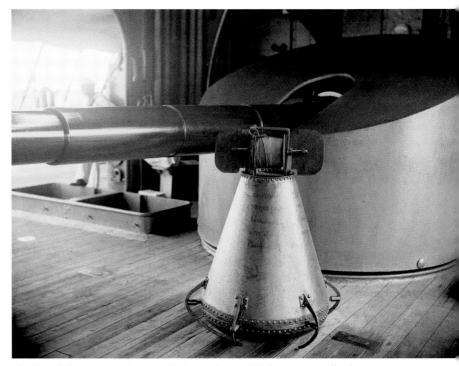

The Spanish Bustamente mine that caught on USS *Texas'* propeller but failed to explode in Guantanamo Bay, June 1898. (Library of Congress)

by Admiral Heihachiro Togo at the battle of Tsushima in 1905 and the issues arising from it. These issues included the effectiveness of large-calibre guns relative to medium-calibre guns in battle. Additionally, the conference reviewed the design of HMS *Dreadnought,* commissioned in 1906 with all big guns and turbine engines. The conference agreed that new U.S. battleships were to be of the "dreadnought" type, but with larger main guns than both the standard 12 inches of current U.S. battleships and those of the follow-on dreadnoughts of the Royal Navy.

The issue of a battleship with an all-big-gun armament had been discussed within the Navy in 1902, and subsequent articles in the U.S. Naval Institute *Proceedings* had highlighted the dangers of not pursuing this concept. This debate led to the ordering in March 1905 (the month after HMS *Dreadnought*) of USS *South Carolina* and USS *Michigan*, the first dreadnoughts for the U.S. Navy. These two battleships carried eight 12-inch guns on 17,900-ton hulls and were capable of 18.5 knots. With their four main gun turrets all on the centerline, with two turrets higher than the other two and "superfiring" over them, these ships were significantly ahead of their time.

In addition to the mandate that future battleships be armed with yet larger guns, the conference also addressed the bureau issue. The General Board of the Navy was instructed to establish the design needs of future battleships and then oversee the early stages of designs before detailed work commenced. A new USS *Texas* and her sister ship USS *New York* were to be the first battleships that benefited from this new structure.

DESIGN CRITERIA

In the process of determining the design requirements for USS *Texas*, several overriding factors were identified. With the nation's increased territorial responsibilities and maritime trade to protect and promote, the new ships had to be able to steam from the West Coast to Manila in the Philippines. To make this journey the ships required engines reliable enough for long distances, plus sufficient coal reserves. The size and weight of the new 14-inch guns and ammunition and of the large battery of twenty-one 5-inch guns required an increase in displacement. The development of dreadnought fleets by the Royal Navy and other European and South American navies required that U.S. dreadnoughts be able to defeat in combat dreadnoughts comparable to themselves.

ALL THIS GAVE USS *TEXAS* THE FOLLOWING PROFILE:

Displacement:	27,000 tons
Length:	573 feet
Beam:	95 feet, 6 inches
Draft:	29 feet
Engines:	two 4-cylinder, vertical, inverted triple-expansion steam engines
Boilers:	14 Babcock and Wilcox coal-fired water-tube boilers
Ship shaft horsepower:	28,000
Speed:	21 knots
Endurance:	7,060 nautical miles at 10 knots
Fuel capacity:	1,900 tons of coal, 267 tons of fuel oil
Armament:	10 x 14-inch/45-calibre main guns in five 2-gun turrets;
	21 x 5-inch/51 secondary battery; 4 x 21-inch submerged torpedo tubes
Armor protection:	Main belt 12 to 10 inches; lower casement 11–9-inch; upper casement 6.5 inch;
	armor deck 2 inch; turret face 14 inch, top 4 inch, sides 2 inch, rear 8 inch;
	barbettes 10- and 12 inch; conning tower 12 inch, top 4 inches.
Complement:	58 officers. 994 sailors

USS *Texas*, in terms of displacement, was over 50 percent larger than the first U.S. dreadnought, USS *South Carolina*. The 14-inch guns of *Texas* were carried forward to the nine dreadnoughts that followed, as well as to in USS *New York*, her sister ship. This gave the U.S. Navy a dreadnought battle line that was not only very powerful but "homogeneous"—all 14-inch-gun battleships.

CONSTRUCTION

The new battleship *Texas* being formed at Newport News Shipbuilding, early 1911. (NARA)

USS *Texas* was built by Newport News Shipbuilding and Dry Dock Company (NNS) at Newport News, Virginia. Situated on the James River, NNS had built seven of the predreadnought battleships of the Great White Fleet. NNS signed the contract to build USS *Texas* on 17 December 1910, with a completion date of 17 December 1913. The contract price was $5,830,000.

The following chronology details the timing of construction.

Plans and specifications delivered to NNS	12/24/1910	Rudder installed	5/14/1912
First hull material ordered	12/27/1910	USS *Texas* launched	5/18/1912
Ship lines faired in mould loft	1/16/1911	USS *Texas* towed from NNS shipyard	
Hull material received	1/19/1911	to Norfolk Navy Yard	9/3/1912
Keel laid	4/17/1911	First gun turret installed	2/22/1913
First frame erected	4/21/1911	First 14-in gun installed	3/5/1913
First transverse bulkhead erected	5/5/1911	First 5-in gun installed	8/5/1913
First large casting for sternpost erected	8/5/1911	Last armor plate installed	3/10/1913
First armor plate for central armor received	8/7/1911	Official sea trial	10/21–29/1913
First compartment tested	9/14/1911	Final inclining experiment	2/21/1914
First armor plate installed as central armor	10/7/1911	USS *Texas* commissioned at NNNS	3/12/1914

Stern view of USS *Texas* under construction, early 1911. Note wooden scaffolding and supports for hull framework. (NARA)

USS *Texas* was an integral part of the "dreadnought race" to build bigger and more heavily armed battleships. In this context, the all-big-gun battleship was the measure by which nations and their navies were evaluated. For USS *Texas* the new 14-inch gun was paramount. The Royal Navy had selected a new 13.5-inch gun for the *Orion* class of dreadnoughts rather than the previously standard 12-inch gun. *Orion* was ordered in the 1909 Royal Navy program, and building commenced in November 1909. Along with the 13.5-inch gun, *Orion* had the first centerline and superfiring gun turret structure in the Royal Navy dreadnought era. Subsequently all Royal Navy battleships followed this arrangement, as originally introduced by USS *South Carolina* (1910).

The 14-inch guns and gun turrets for *Texas* were built by Bethlehem Steel. The prototype 14-inch gun was first fired in January 1910. The uniform results of its testing period enabling the order for the ship to proceed in December 1910.

The 14-inch gun fired a 1,400-pound shell with a bursting charge of 31.5 pounds for armor piercing. The guns could elevate to a maximum of 15 degrees and had a range of 23,000 yards. Shells were stored face down in the shell room. Each in turn would be connected to a winch at a padeye inserted into its base, hoisted to a monorail, moved to the lower projectile hoist, and then sent up to the upper handling room. There it was transferred to the upper projectile hoist, which delivered the shell to the gun house, where the padeye was removed and the shell transferred to a tray connected to the gun's breach for ramming.

Four powder, or propellant, bags totaling 405 pounds fired the shell. These charges were held in powder tanks stored in the magazine on the same deck as the shell room. The bags were removed from the tanks, passed by hand through a scuttle from the magazine to the central handling room and then, again by hand, in the powder hoist. This hoist elevated the bags to a powder flat at

The hull of dreadnought *Texas* is now well formed. Note sailing ship in right background. (NARA)

Fourteen-inch guns and gun turret being assembled at Bethlehem Steel. (NARA)

TEXAS.

the base of the gun house where they were hand-passed up to the gun crew, who laid the bags onto the tray for ramming into the breach.

Dreadnought designers worked to the principle that the ship needed to be protected by armor against gunfire equal in power to that of its own guns. Improved treatment and production of armor plate, more powerful optics and propellant, and the rapidly increasing range of torpedoes all served to increase the distance at which battleships needed to fight if they were to survive. The armor design had to deal with shells fired both at relatively close range with nearly horizontal trajectories and from longer range with a steeper angle of fall.

USS *Texas* carried 6,738 tons of Class A armor. Class A armor had been face-hardened by carbon and heat during the manufacturing process. This armor was supplied by Bethlehem (2,257 tons), Carnegie Steel (2,207 tons), and Midvale Steel (2,744 tons). The armor was installed on vertical surfaces as follows: hull, 2,944 tons; turrets, 640 tons; barbettes, 2,077 tons; conning tower, 222 tons. This armor had to defeat shells hitting the ship at or near the perpendicular to its surface. The front layer of the armor plate was designed to break the nose of the shell and deform the body, while the more elastic body of the armor plate beneath prevented penetration.

Class B armor was used for all horizontal surfaces. This armor was not face-hardened and was found in testing to be more effective in deflecting a shell with an oblique angle of impact.

USS *Texas* initially carried twenty-one 5-inch guns. Nineteen 5-inch guns were located along the second deck in casements and two on the first superstructure (or 01) deck. One second-deck gun was at the extreme after end of the ship, the "tail stinger." In this role the 5-inch gun could be hand-fed to deliver a high rate of fire of eight to ten rounds per minute. Each shell weighed 50 pounds. The separate propellant charge weighed 24.5 pounds. Shells and propellant were delivered by a hoist from a magazine located below the magazine that served the 14-inch guns. A 5-inch gun required an 11-man crew.

This large battery of 5-inch guns was required to counter the increase in size and speed of torpedo-carrying craft. Destroyers displacing on the order of 1,000 tons could carry torpedoes, in addition to a modest-sized gun. Just as important, destroyers could exceed 30 knots and attack from behind smoke screens or at night. Torpedo speeds of 30 knots or more meant that time available for the gun crew to react, acquire the target, set the range, load, and commence and continue fire diminished rapidly. It was noted that the Japanese navy used destroyer torpedo attacks to great effect during the Russo-Japanese War of 1904–1905.

USS *Texas* in dry-dock showing port screw now fitted and cut out (MW) at stern for rear 5-inch gun, the "tail stinger." (NARA)

As for propulsion, the two four-cylinder reciprocating steam engines that powered USS *Texas* were built in place by NNS. Each engine had its own space, positioned side by side in a mirror-image layout. A watertight bulkhead separated the engines; it extended from the third deck down to the mid-part of the engine room, where it connected to a centerline wiring passage. The engine rooms were each 60 feet long and just under 27 feet wide, which provided sufficient space for future installation of turbine engines, provided they could attain the range required.

Initially, turbines similar to those installed in the *Delaware*, *Florida*, and *Wyoming* classes of dreadnoughts (except for USS *Delaware* herself, which had reciprocating steam engines) had been specified for *Texas* and *New York*. The design was changed to reciprocating engines because the turbine manufacturers, Curtis and Parsons, could not meet the Navy's range specifications, which was beyond their design capabilities. The Navy required 7,060 nautical miles, but the manufacturers would only agree to 5,605 nautical miles, less than the distance from the West Coast to Manila. In a trial USS *Delaware* had steamed for 24 hours at full speed without an engine breakdown. A new technique of forced oil lubrication through a closed circuit from the main-bearing supply pipe to the top of the connecting rod underpinned such reliability. Additionally, the new standard of securing all bolt heads reduced vibration and loosening of bolts. Accordingly, *Texas* and *New York* were ordered with reciprocating steam engines rather than turbines. These engines drove two shafts and attached propellers.

The four-cylinder structure expanded the steam from the boilers through a high-pressure cylinder, from which the steam flowed to an intermediate-pressure cylinder and thence to two low-pressure cylinders (rather than a very large single low-pressure cylinder). Each cylinder drove a piston with a stroke of 48 inches that in turn drove the propeller shaft with a three-bladed propeller. Each engine was rated at 14,050 horsepower, and together they propelled the ship at a maximum speed of 21 knots.

The engine room was located between the mid-deck gun-turret magazines and the aft superfiring turret.

The 14 Babcock and Wilcox water-tube boilers that provided steam at 295 psi and 417 degrees for the engines were located in four fire rooms situated amidships. The steam lines from the boilers to the engine rooms passed outboard of the longitudinal bulkhead around the midships magazine to avoid heating the magazine and degrading the propellant inside.

The boilers were fed coal from bunkers located along the sides of the machinery spaces. These spaces sat between the longitudinal bulkheads extending through the second and third decks as well as the lower bunkers. Besides coal, the ship also carried 247 tons of fuel oil, to be sprayed on the coal to increase combustion when needed.

USS *Texas* was fitted with an armored conning tower for command and control. The tower was aft of number-two superfiring turret, five feet above the 02 level for visibility to the bow over the two forward gun turrets.

View of stern section from cage mast before installation of rear turrets. (Texas Parks & Wildlife Department)

The tower had 12-inch-thick armored sides and, as previously mentioned, weighed 222 tons. This weight was carried by multiple bulkheads extending down five decks to the central station on the armored deck. The tower had five viewing slits across the front and three on each side. Within the tower, a front section was for speed and steering; an aft section handled fire control.

The deckhouse, located one level below and aft of the conning tower, was divided among the admiral's stateroom, his cabin (which spread around the conning tower), quarters for the admiral's chief of staff, and a "flag" galley. The deckhouse was the base for the forward cage mast. A small, covered bridge, which also served as the signal bridge, was fitted on the forward side of the forward cage mast, immediately behind but above the conning tower.

Also aft of number-two turret was the 01-level deckhouse, for the captain's suite and two 5-inch guns, port and starboard. This deckhouse extended to just short of turret number three. The uptakes for the two funnels passed through the deckhouse, which was the base for the two funnels themselves.

Two boat cranes, one port and one starboard, were just forward of the after funnel on the main deck. The ship's boats were carried in slings alongside both funnels.

The cage masts were composed of an open weave of sets of tubes clamped to each other where they crossed. Additionally, circumferential tubes were added to form rings and triangles within the cage and clamped to the vertical tubes where they met. This feature created rigidity for the mast and provided the base for platforms. Wire gratings were set as landings for the ladders to the searchlight levels and the spotting platform at the top of the mast. This spotting platform carried a range finder, which needed to be at the highest level possible. The cage mast also carried yardarms for signaling and antenna for the radios. The weave design of the masts minimized the explosive impact of shells: its open nature dissipated the pressure of the expanding gasses from high-explosive (HE) shells and made it less likely that the fuse action of armor-piercing shells would be triggered.

The two cage masts carried two searchlights each. The forward mast carried the searchlights on its forward side, with one higher than the other. The aft mast carried the searchlights on its aft side in a similar vertical arrangement.

The main weather deck ran the length of the ship and was 55 feet above the keel at the bow, sloping down to 47 feet above the keel just prior to the stern, where it was cut away to the second deck to form a casement for the stern's tail stinger. The second deck was eight feet below the main deck until it reached the uptakes, aft of which it sloped down so that it was ten feet below the main deck for the remainder of its length. Forward of the armored bulkhead for the forward 5-inch guns, the second deck was reserved for the ship's officers. The dividing bulkhead created space for ten casements for port and starboard 5-inch guns between number-two and -three barbettes (cylindrical structures containing the ammunitions-handling machinery for the main-battery guns and supporting their rotating gun houses). Here also was berthing and messing space for the crew. Between the port and starboard casements were longitudinal passageways, funnel uptakes, boiler evaporators, and the "mess decks," the crew's cafeteria. Aft of the casements and against the hull were separate spaces for the dental clinic, barber shop, laundry, and sick bay. Around the barbettes for number-three and -four gun turrets was more crew berthing. The deck here could be removed for access to the third-deck and lower engine spaces. Farthest aft were crew washrooms and heads, plus the one 5-inch gun.

The third deck was 31 feet above the keel for its entire length. Crew spaces extended to the aft end of number-five turret barbette. The space aft of number-five turret was reserved for chief petty officer berthing and messing arrangements. Amidships and below the casements were coal bunkers alongside the hull, plus longitudinal ammunition passageways and uptake spaces. Forward of the casements were storerooms.

The third deck represented the last line of armored defense against incoming, plunging shells. The armored deck plate was specially treated steel created by Carnegie in 1910. This steel was rolled in the open-hearth process, alloyed with nickel, chrome, and vanadium. This created a homogeneous plate able to deflect shells with an oblique angle of attack. The armor plate for both the second and third decks was an inch and three-quarters thick.

Below the third deck were the magazines and shell rooms for the five 14-inch gun turrets and the engine and boiler rooms. In the aft section below the armored deck, an additional armored deck was sloped down to the stern to cover the steering gear.

Below the deck carrying the boilers, engine room, and magazines was an inner bottom that ran the entire length between the various tanks that held feed water, fresh water, and oil. This inner bottom followed the hull up the sides to the third deck. This design formed a foundation for the hull-mounted armor plates. Additionally, the structure created in effect a second hull shell. Inboard from the double-hull sides was a longitudinal torpedo bulkhead an inch and a half thick. This bulkhead was also the inbound side of the coal bunkers.

FITTING OUT

USS *Texas*, gathering way down the slipway.
(Library of Congress)

Twenty-five hundred workmen went on board when USS *Texas* entered the fitting-out dock at the Norfolk Navy Yard; they were to turn the raw hull into a fighting ship. In addition to building and installing the engines and boilers, they constructed cage masts, cranes, secondary and main armament, the conning tower with a bridge and charthouse, and two 8-ton anchors.

Texas was ready for the builder's trials on 19 October 1913, when she left Newport News for the coast of Maine. These trials, which commenced on 23 October, subjected the engines and hull to a series of demanding tests to ensure the ship was capable of meeting her designed speed. They had to determine what steam pressures were required to drive the propellers at the revolutions per minute needed to achieve her top speed. USS *Texas* completed these trials, establishing that an engine speed of 124 revolutions per minute produced the design top speed of 21 knots.

The commissioning of USS *Texas* took place at the Norfolk Navy Yard at 12:30 p.m. on Thursday, 12 March. Captain A. W. Grant took command of the ship before 800 sailors massed on the broad deck aft of number-three gun turret. A large component of the sailors were from the old battleship USS *Idaho*, which had recently been sold to Greece; the *Idaho* sailors had sailed their ship there and returned to the United States by a transport. There followed a period of settling the crew and ship into a fully functional member of the fleet, complete with stores, ammunition, and coal.

The crew swung their hammocks from billet hooks attached to deck heads. Mess tables and benches were also stored overhead, lowered three times a day for the meals, delivered by running mess cooks from the galley. A key feature of USS *Texas* was that her whole crew was thrown together daily as the men moved about the ship to the washrooms, heads, canteen, hammock nettings, scuttlebutts, and laundry. Coaling produced a

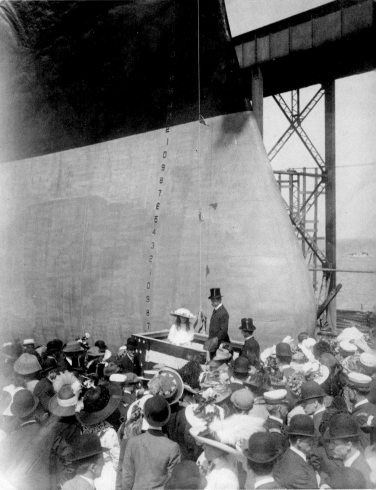

Program for the launching ceremony of USS *Texas*, 18 May 1912. (Texas Parks & Wildlife Department)

(Left) Miss Claudia Lyon, daughter of Texas Republican Cecil Lyon, christening USS *Texas* with champagne. (Library of Congress) (Right) Miss Claudia Lyon and party on launching platform, at the bow. (Texas Parks & Wildlife Department)

UNITED STATES NAVAL INSTITUTE

very dirty crew and ship at days' end, and the rush to clean the ship and the sailors was a major event.

COALING SHIP

The first coaling of USS *Texas* took place in Hampton Roads, where the ironclads *Virginia* (the old *Merrimac*) and USS *Monitor* had fought in 1862. The ship anchored under the guns of Fort Monroe, and a tug brought out two coal barges, one for each side, filled with a total of 1,700 tons of coal. Sailors and officers together shoveled the coal in the barges into canvas bags, which sixteen booms hoisted up to the weather deck. There the bags were dragged to the 28 chutes and their coal was dumped, falling into the 21 bunkers several decks below, where more sailors spread the coal into even layers.

At four in the afternoon the mess cooks served up thick corned-beef sandwiches and coffee. The coaling went on to late that night. The crew was encouraged both by the ship's band on top of a gun turret and by fierce competition, egged on by the ship's officers, between the crews unloading the two coal barges. When the coaling was finished the exhausted crew washed up and sat at their mess tables, where they were fed thick soup, large slices of bread and "slum," the cook's version of slumgullion, a hearty mixture of macaroni, chopped meat, and ketchup.

The next day the ship steamed out into the Atlantic and used seawater to remove what remained of the coal dust that had coated the ship. The crew wanted USS *Texas* to look smart for the entry into her designated home port, New York.

All this time, effort, and expense was invested in USS *Texas* to enable the U.S. Navy to place her ten 14-inch guns where it wanted them to protect the United States and its interests.

View of USS *Texas*' starboard quarter just prior to launch. Note the inclined walkway with mules carrying building materials. (Library of Congress)

USS *Texas* entering the water of the James River. (Library of Congress)

USS *Texas* pierside at Norfolk Navy Yard for fitting out. Note the light-colored strake just aft the bow section where the main armor is still to be fitted. (NARA)

USS *Texas* in Dry-Dock Number 3 during outfitting, April 1913. (NARA)

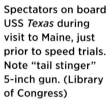

Spectators on board USS *Texas* during visit to Maine, just prior to speed trials. Note "tail stinger" 5-inch gun. (Library of Congress)

USS *Texas* at 21.792 knots during Run 24 on 27 October 1913. Note thick coal smoke from two funnels. (NARA)

The Democratic Banner.

$1.50 PER YEAR   MT. VERNON, OHIO, TUESDAY, APRIL 21, 1914—No. 32   ESTABLISHED 1836

REFUSES TO ORDER A SALUTE

The Answer To President Wilson's Ultimatum

Huerta Boldly Defies United States.

QUICK ACTION LIKELY

Ports of Tampico and Vera Cruz Will Be Seized.

FLEET POSTED BY WIRELESS

Defiance of Mexican Dictator Comes After a Day of Haggling by Him, and After President Wilson Had Again Served Notice That Demand For Salute Was Unconditional—Order Expected For the Blockading and Seizure of Ports On the East and West Coasts of Mexico.

Washington, April 20.—Huerta has defied the United States and refused to order a salute of apology to the American flag. That is his answer to President Wilson's ultimatum.

CAPTAIN CLEAVES INSPECTING U. S. S. TEXAS, NOW BEING RUSHED INTO COMMISSION, AND FEDERAL BUILDING IN VERA CRUZ

1: INSPECTING the TEXAS — 2: FEDERAL BUILDING of VERA CRUZ

ACTIVITY IS SHOWN

Along The Line In Ohio National Guard

Prepared to Do Its Part In Meeting Mexican Situation.

ENLISTMENTS MOVE RAPIDLY

Attainment of Required Strength For Hostilities and Drilling and Equipment of Men Would Require a Comparatively Short Time — Adjutant General Wood and Other Officers Ready to Meet Any Eventuality.

GEORGE H. WOOD

Ohio's Adjutant General Keenly Interested In Mexican Situation.

TESTS THIS WEEK FOR SCHOOL JOBS

Important Examinations to Be Conducted By Board.

(pictured center) Captain Cleaves inspecting USS *Texas* just prior to commissioning. (Library of Congress)

Officers, crew, and Marines march aboard USS *Texas* for commissioning ceremony, 12 March 1914 at the Norfolk Navy Yard. Note the Salvation Army horse-drawn wagon serving hot coffee and doughnuts on a cold, snow-covered pier. (Texas Parks & Wildlife Department)

MEXICAN ADVENTURES

During 1913, the United States became involved in an interesting aspect of naval diplomacy, one that in due course would involve USS *Texas*. The Mexican Revolution, which commenced in 1910 had a complex history and multiple characters, came to a head on 19 February 1913 when Victoriano Huerta became president of Mexico after murdering the elected incumbent. Woodrow Wilson, who became president of the United States on 4 March 1913, declined to recognize Huerta and embargoed arms shipments to his army, while allowing arms to be shipped to Huerta's opponent Venustiano Carranza. A difficult interlude ensued that lasted until 6 April 1914. On this day USS *Dolphin*, one of the original "ABCD ships" of 1883, sent a landing party of seven sailors ashore at Tampico, a Mexican port on the Gulf of Mexico, for supplies. Tampico was under martial law, and the Mexican army had orders to arrest any attempt to dock. A junior Mexican officer arrested the seven American sailors and a paymaster and took them to his superior officer. This officer promptly returned them to *Dolphin* and sent a more senior officer to explain the incident and express regret. Unfortunately, Admiral Henry Mayo, under whose command USS *Dolphin* was, demanded within 24 hours a 21-gun salute of the American flag as an apology.

President Huerta was able to avoid the salute and the time limit by arguing that the United States could not make demands of a government that it did not recognize; in any case, he asserted, the craft that had brought the sailors ashore was not flying a flag, so the flag had not

View of U.S. fleet at Veracruz from USS *Texas*, her crew at rest. (Texas Parks & Wildlife Department)

been insulted. This diplomatic to-and-fro lasted until 20 April, as the Navy stood by ready to blockade and occupy Veracruz, a larger port about 240 miles south.

In the hours before dawn on the 21st, President Wilson was wakened by a telephone call from the Secretary of State William Jennings Bryan advising him that a Hamburg-America steamer, *Ypiranga*, from Germany was about to dock at Veracruz to unload a large shipment of arms and ammunition. Furthermore, three trains were waiting at the pier to load and transport the arms to President Huerta. Secretary of the Navy Josephus Daniels too was plugged into the telephone conversation. The three of them, in their pajamas, conferred, and at length Wilson instructed Daniels to order Admiral Frank Friday Fletcher, commanding the U.S. fleet off the Mexican Gulf coast, to "Take Veracruz at once." This "Pajama Conference" launched the American invasion of Mexico.

On 21 April Admiral Fletcher gave the order for U.S. Marines and sailors to land at Veracruz. In the three days of fighting the Mexican army and civilians, twenty-two U.S. Marines and sailors were killed and seventy wounded. Worse, *Ypiranga*, prevented from unloading her cargo for President Huerta at Veracruz, sailed on to Puerto Mexico (modern-day Coatzacoalcos), where she unloaded it unmolested. Admiral Fletcher was ordered to apologize to the captain of the *Ypiranga*, as a result of a German note of protest to the State Department pointing out that the interference with *Ypiranga* had occurred without prior declaration of a blockade or state of war.

On the 25th the battleship USS *Mississippi* off Veracruz put into the water a flying boat with the mission of determining the position of the Mexican opponents of the landing party Admiral Fletcher had sent. The flying boat flew two successful reconnaissance flights over Veracruz, earning the commendation of the admiral.

While these events were occurring in Veracruz, USS *Texas* was in her home port of New York. On 12 May 1914 her crew took part in a march down Broadway as far as City Hall, part of a ceremony with children commemorating the deaths of the 22 Marines and

USS *Texas* entering New York Harbor attended by three tugs on the way to the Navy yard, 27 March 1914. (Library of Congress)

sailors at Veracruz. The crew then marched to Brooklyn and the New York Navy Yard for the funeral service, attended by President Wilson and Secretary of State Bryan. During the service USS *Texas* Marines fired three volleys over the graves in salute.

Texas left New York on 15 May and sailed to the Gulf of Mexico to anchor off Veracruz as part of the blockading force. This force comprised USS *Connecticut*, *Michigan*, *South Carolina*, *New York*, *Wyoming*, *Arkansas*, *Florida*, and *Minnesota*. USS *Texas* remained on this post until 8 August, when she sailed for New York, the Mexican affair having come to a partial conclusion. Huerta was removed from the presidency in 1914 by Venustiano Carranza and left Mexico on 17 July on board the German cruiser *Dresden* to exile in Spain. However, not all the other ships off Veracruz left; the Mexican presidential succession was unresolved, other candidates continuing their campaigns with arms, requiring naval presence in the Gulf of Mexico. The occupation of Veracruz continued until the U.S. Army withdrew on 23 November 1914. Carranza became president of Mexico in May 1917.

While these events were incurring in Mexico, in Europe Archduke Ferdinand, heir to the Austro-Hungarian Habsburg emperor Franz Josef, was assassinated on 28 June 1914, and events began to spiral out of control. Continental European nations, together with Russia and Great Britain, found that alliances they had made were creating a difficult environment. Political and diplomatic mismanagement resulted in a war that rapidly spread around the world. While the United States remained neutral, it quickly found a role as a major supplier of arms to France, Great Britain, and Russia. However, the United States was unable to supply arms to Germany, owing to a Royal Navy blockade of Germany. German interest in Mexico and the volatile U.S.-Mexican relationship suggested to German diplomats based in the United States that an outbreak of war between the two could lead to a reduction in arms available from the United States for the allies. To this end German diplomats and agents in the United States and Mexico set out to disrupt American arms shipments to the allies.

USS *Texas* left New York on 5 September 1914 and took part in Atlantic Fleet training, exercises, and

USS *Texas* taking on coal from a coaling ship at Veracruz, May 1914. (Texas Parks & Wildlife Department)

After coaling ship, USS *Texas* crew members enjoy a hearty meal of "slumgullion" on the quarterdeck. Note the coal dust and the blackened attire of the men. (Texas Parks & Wildlife Department)

gunnery drills off the East Coast. In mid-September, the ship returned to the Gulf of Mexico and cruised between Veracruz, the Sacrificios Islands, Tuxpam, and Tampico. On 6 November USS *Texas* entered the port of Galveston on a goodwill visit, an opportunity for Texans to visit and inspect their ship. The more formal aspect of the stay was the presentation of a silver service by Governor Oscar Colquitt to Captain Albert Grant at a civic ceremony.

After a stay of seven days the ship returned to duty off the Gulf coast of Mexico, specifically at Lobos Island, where the crew repaired and manned the lighthouse. The uncluttered waters of the area enabled the officers and crew to run the ship through a series of exercises to determine fully how USS *Texas* performed. The anchor was raised every morning and the ship run in circles at various speeds and rudder angles, to make the crew knowledgeable in maneuvers to avoid torpedoes.

In the five gun turrets, the seventy men in each were distributed among the various levels and activities of their barbettes, from the magazine to hoists, handling rooms, and the loading of guns for firing. These steps each required the handling a 14-inch shell weighing three-quarters of a ton and four powder bags collectively weighing 420 pounds, up from the previously mentioned 405 pounds when the process for formulating the powder changed. All this required precise timing and deft movement, as the shell and powder bags shifted with the ship's motion. Other exercises involved man-overboard, damage control, and fire drills, as well as simulated collision, underwater damage, and flooding.

These exercises lasted until 20 December 1914, when USS *Texas* sailed for New York and the navy yard for repairs and maintenance. In February 1915, the ship rejoined the Atlantic Fleet. In the early hours of 25 May, USS *Texas* was alerted by radio that the Holland America liner *Ryndam* had been rammed by another vessel. The memory of the *Titanic* disaster still fresh, USS *Texas*, *South Carolina*, *Louisiana*, and *Michigan* rushed at top speed to the scene, just south of the Nantucket Shoals, to assist in the rescue the 230 passengers. There were no casualties, and the liner was escorted by USS *Texas* to the Holland America terminal in New York. The Holland America Line expressed its gratitude to the USS *Texas* by another addition to the ship's silver service, a model of the famous Dutch flagship of Admiral Michiel de Ruyter.

(right) Captain Grant receiving a gift of a silver service from Governor Oscar Colquitt of Texas, Galveston, 7 November 1914. (Texas Parks & Wildlife Department)

(below) Ammunition barge alongside USS *Texas*, 14-inch shells being hoisted using padeyes. (Texas Parks & Wildlife Department)

U.S. Atlantic Fleet with USS *Texas* leading in 1917. (Library of Congress)

A SENSE OF THE FUTURE

In 1916, USS *Texas* berthed at the New York Navy Yard, where two critical additions were made to the ship. The first was the installation of 3-inch guns on top of the boat cranes. These guns, initially referred to as "sky guns," were seen as a defense against flying boats, seaplanes, and powered balloons. The U.S. Navy had explored the use of aircraft in a naval context with flights by Eugene Ely in 1910 and 1911 from and to USS *Birmingham* and *Pennsylvania*. The recent use of a flying boat from USS *Mississippi* over Veracruz demonstrated how greatly aerial spotting and reconnaissance could aid naval missions.

A naval air station had been established at Pensacola, Florida, to train naval pilots. A catapult was built on board the armored cruiser USS *North Carolina*, stationed at Pensacola; trials demonstrated that aircraft could be successfully launched from a ship. American naval attachés at the American embassies in London and Berlin monitored the naval war. Therefore, the U.S. Navy was well aware of seaplane activity in the battles in the North Sea, the Dardanelles, and Baltic, as well as the scouting activities of German naval zeppelins over the North Sea.

The installation of antiaircraft (sky) guns on USS *Texas*, the first on any U.S. Navy ship, opened the subject of how to defend ships from air attack: locating, tracking, and calculating the aiming point of a rapidly moving target in three dimensions. These questions would be effectively addressed only in the 1940s with the marrying of radar, fire control, fuses, and automatic weapons with very high rates of fire.

The second addition was made in July, when Hannibal Ford, a private citizen and owner of the Ford Instrument Company, brought aboard USS *Texas* a prototype Ford "range keeper" and demonstrated its workings to a group of gunnery officers. The range keeper was housed in a box with a glass face containing a series of dials; attached to the sides of the box were numerous handles that moved the dials when turned. The dials indicated the range to the target, its bearing, ship's speed, target speed, wind direction, and the needed angle of deflection. The box stood on a pedestal attached to the deck. This new instrument was the latest attempt at a disciplined, reliable, and measurable means to address the technical core of fire control—where to point the guns and at what range to fire them so as to hit the target.

At the battle of Manila Bay in May 1898, prior to the Ford range keeper, Lieutenant Bradley Fiske had directed the fire of his ship, the gunboat USS *Petrel*, while tied 45 feet up her foremast. Using his own invention, the "stadimeter," to find the range to the target, he called the information down to the captain on the bridge. As the Spanish warships were at anchor, changes simply reflected the movement of the observing ship. At the battle of Santiago, in the same conflict, a gunnery officer stood on top of a gun turret and called as to target position and directions down to the gun captain. While these battles were overwhelming victories for the U.S. Navy, they showed that the inaccuracy of naval gunfire was a major concern. At Manila Bay, only 2.5 percent of shells fired had hit their stationary targets. For Santiago, where the Spanish ships had been steaming at high speed and American ships had chased them on approximately parallel courses, gunnery accuracy was 1.3 percent.

The issue of determining the range to the target had been studied for many years, growing out of the use of telescopes by field artillery. In the 1880s Lieutenant Fiske had attempted to create an electrical range finder for use on board a ship, as well as a telescopic sight for a 6-inch gun. His stadimeter resulted from his awareness that an easy-to-use instrument was needed during the heat and pressure of battle. In 1889 the Royal Navy noted Lieutenant Fiske's efforts and, spurred on by them, established in 1892 a committee on naval range finders. Subsequently the Admiralty selected the Barr and Stroud range finder for the Royal Navy; it entered service in 1899. The U.S. Navy also adopted Barr and Stroud range finders.

The next issue was how to determine where a moving target would be in the future, given that the shell once fired would take some amount of time to reach it. An early attempt to address this problem was the creation of a trigonometric slide-rule-type calculator by Lt. John Saumarez Dumaresq, RN, in 1902. This instrument, referred to as "a Dumaresq," could calculate the rate of movement of a target ship within a few seconds. This instrument would go through multiple variations and would ultimately underpin increasingly sophisticated Royal Navy fire-control instruments.

In early 1901 Lieutenant William Sims of the U.S. Navy met Captain Percy Scott of the Royal Navy in Hong Kong. This was a fortuitous meeting. Lieutenant Sims had been complaining about the inaccurate gunnery of his service, whereas Captain Scott had significantly improved the gunnery of his own with his continuous-aim telescopic gunsight. Notwithstanding the differences in their ranks and navies, Captain Scott shared with Sims his techniques. Sims was able over time to bring new methods, techniques, and equipment into use in the U.S. Navy, and its gunnery improved.

As armored cruisers and battleships grew larger and were more heavily armed and the range of torpedoes increased, fire control became even more important. A significant development occurred in 1907 when Lieutenant Commander Joseph Reeves and Lieutenant Richard White, gunnery officers on board USS *Wisconsin*, built a range and deflection transmitter as the first step of building a fire-control instrument that would automatically measure the rate of change of the range to target. This instrument, a

Prototype Ford range keeper on stand. (U.S. Naval Academy)

Dumaresq's original fire-control instrument, 1902. (Judi Burr)

"range projector," was trialed on USS *Virginia* and then installed across the fleet in 1909.

In 1908 the U.S. Navy acquired Vickers "range clocks" as adjuncts to range finders. They showed what range should be input to gunsights at any given interval, the rate of increase or decrease in the range due to the speed of either the target or firing ship having been ascertained by range finder and timing, spotting, or range projector. The instrument consisted essentially of a dial face, a movable pointer, and a speed-adjusting index, and it was effective at ranges from 2,000 to 14,000 yards.

Lieutenant Sims was appointed naval aide to President Roosevelt in November 1907, and this position, together with his role as inspector of target practice, enabled him to make further impacts on the Navy, including contributing to the decision to arm the second USS *Texas* with 14-inch guns.

The emergence of the all-big-gun dreadnought and the torpedo made the need for long-range gunnery paramount. As gun ranges lengthened from 2,000 yards to 10,000 yards and beyond, shells no longer flew in flat, horizontal trajectories and so were exposed to additional physical forces. In addition, because it was important that all guns firing be aimed at the same target, individual gunlaying became a thing of the past, replaced by salvo firing. Lieutenant Fiske in 1890, serving on board USS *Baltimore*, envisaged "director firing"—person elevated above the guns sighting the target and controlling the training and firing of all the broadside guns together. At the time, the mechanisms and equipment necessary did not yet exist, but later Percy Scott, now an admiral, began working with Vickers Ltd., a British shipbuilder and armament manufacturer, to design and build a director. It was trialed on board HMS *Neptune* in 1910. Admiral Scott and now-Captain Sims maintained their friendship and continued sharing gunnery information.

When USS *Texas* was launched and fitted out, she had, in addition to a "spotting top" and range finder on her mainmast, a plotting room on the armored deck with a plotting board and range clocks plus communication links to the gun turrets to control train, elevation, and firing. In 1910 the U.S. Navy ordered a gyrocompass from Sperry Gyroscope to support the plotting board; the repeater function of the gyrocompass could be used to transmit fire-control information from

After coaling, scrub and wash clothes. (Texas Parks & Wildlife Department)

input manually to the Ford range keeper. A plotting-room officer input an estimate of target course. The range keeper then continually compared the observed spotting-top data with the estimated inputs from the plotting room until they merged. At that point the range keeper could determine the present range of the target and project where the target would be in the future.

This comparison of observed and estimated data was an ongoing process, because changes in the target's course caused calculated and observed courses and speeds to diverge; succeeding observations and estimates would determine a new firing solution. This continuous updating of the firing solution was achieved by a new internal calculating mechanism, the "Ford integrator." Ford had improved on the existing mechanical integrator, based on measuring the rotation of a small ball, by eliminating slippage through the use of double balls and stronger springs on a cylinder bracket that held them in place. The result was highly accurate integration plus the ability to drive smoothly other components of the range keeper.

The trials of the Ford range keeper on board USS *Texas* were highly successful, and the Navy ordered a large number of units of a modified design, referred to as the "Ford Range Keeper Mark (or Mk) 1." The most evident change between the prototype as trialed and the Mark 1 was the addition of a large dial representing the target ship below the own-ship dial. *Texas* received a Mark 1 to replace the prototype, and in 1917 other battleships began to receive them as well.

The Ford range keeper, an early analog computer, would go through many iterations before the latest version was installed in the 1940s' *Iowa* class of battleships, where they were to see action in World War II, the Korean War, Vietnam, and Desert Storm in 1991.

USS *Texas* remained on the East Coast until January 1917, when she sailed to Guantanamo Bay and then took station for two months in the Gulf of Guacanayabo on the south coast of Cuba There she supported the Cuban government in its conflict with a former president, José Miguel Gómez. On 23 March USS *Texas* sailed for Hampton Roads, arriving on the 27th and proceeding to the York River. From 27 March until 20 August she remained in the Chesapeake Bay, after which she sailed to the New York Navy Yard as part of her preparation for war with Germany.

the spotting top to the plotting room and gun turrets. Director firing was implemented with the introduction of the "directorscope," a periscope-based instrument in the spotting top. The directorscope was first tested on board USS *Michigan* in 1915 and installed on USS *Texas* in the same year.

In 1916, Sperry released a fire-control system based upon a central plotting machine, a "battle tracer," that recorded the courses of both the target and "own ship." From its gunnery officers could anticipate future movements so as to direct their own guns. Hannibal Ford, at the time a Sperry employee, had devised and patented the battle tracer in 1914. A prototype was installed on board USS *New York* for testing in 1915 but was found to be more useful for navigation than for fire control.

With the Ford range keeper, gunnery officers of USS *Texas* could create a mathematical model of the target's track and from that produce a firing solution. The range keeper received own-ship course from a gyrocompass repeater and own-ship speed by manual input, based on propeller revolutions. The spotting-top officers using range finders determined the target's range and bearing, which were transmitted to the plotting room and

WORLD WAR I

President Wilson had adopted a policy of neutrality between the allies and the Central Powers. This policy did not prevent American businesses from selling arms and other materials to combatants. However, the declaration by Germany in February 1915 of unrestricted submarine warfare around the British Isles and the British of embargo on all trade with Germany led to friction between the United States and Great Britain. The naval blockade of Germany included the search and arrest of American ships for goods being carried to Germany that Great Britain had embargoed. This embargo had a major negative impact on cotton and pork prices in the United States, causing farmers to protest to Washington. Germany at first evaded the full impact of the naval blockade by buying American products through companies established in Holland, Denmark, and the Scandinavian countries. Exports from the United States to these countries increased dramatically after 1914.

Wilson responded to both the unrestricted submarine war, especially the sinking of the British liner *Lusitania* with American passengers on board, and the trade embargo by suddenly expressing support in a letter dated 21 July 1915 to Secretary of the Navy Daniels for a "wise and adequate naval program." Wilson's surprise conversion to building up the Navy after

Oil painting by American artist Burnell Poole, *The 6th Battle Squadron of the Grand Fleet Leaving the Firth of Forth* depicting U.S. naval operations in World War I. The composition of the ships of the 6th Battle Squadron during their operational history, appearing in the painting in no particular order were: USS *Delaware*, USS *Florida*, USS *Wyoming*, USS *Arkansas*, USS *New York*, and USS *Texas*. (NHHC)

having restricted its building program since 1912 to two battleships a year, produced in Congress a bill approved on 15 August 1916 to build ten battleships, six battle cruisers, ten scout cruisers, fifty destroyers, sixty-seven submarines, and thirteen auxiliary vessels. Of these, four battleships and four battle cruisers, plus fifty-eight other vessels, were to be built immediately, the balance to be started within three years.

However, President Wilson was unaware of, or ignored, the activities of German secret agents in the United States and Mexico. Agents in the United States were actively sabotaging American factories producing arms and ammunition for the allies and planting time-delayed bombs on ships carrying arms to England and France. German agents established near the White House a germ-warfare laboratory that supplied vials of anthrax and glanders bacteria to agents in Baltimore and New York with which to infect horses waiting to be shipped to Europe. (Horses were the primary motive power for moving guns, equipment, and supplies to the front line.) The most significant act of sabotage was an explosion at the Black Tom ammunition storage facility in New Jersey, on 30 July 1916, powerful enough to blow out a large number of windows in lower Manhattan, that denied the Russian army the arms it needed for its next campaign against the Austro-Hungarian and German armies.

On 31 January 1917 the German ambassador, Johann Heinrich von Bernstorff, advised the U.S. government that Germany would restart its unrestricted submarine warfare campaign, suspended owing to the American reaction to the *Lusitania* sinking, around Great Britain. President Wilson withdrew the American ambassador to Germany, James W. Gerard, and ordered the German ambassador to return home.

That same month the Royal Navy's cryptanalysis office, known as "Room 40," intercepted and decoded a telegram from Arthur Zimmermann, the German foreign secretary, instructing the German ambassador in Mexico to propose that Mexico join with Germany if the United States entered the war. Republished in the United States, the telegram aroused American public opinion; its proviso that Mexico would regain the territories of Texas, New Mexico, and Arizona, especially infuriated those states. President Wilson could not ignore the "Zimmermann Telegram," nor any longer ignore the ongoing sabotage or the recent sinking by U-boat of three U.S. merchant ships.

President Wilson addressed Congress on 2 April 1917, and war was declared against Germany.

It took until November 1917 for the administration to decide to send a division of battleships to join the Royal Navy against Germany. Admiral Sims was sent to London in late March 1917 to open discussions with the Admiralty on the level and areas of cooperation between the U.S. and Royal Navies. The initial focus was on the need for destroyers to combat submarines and for a convoy system to protect merchant shipping. There was strong reluctance in the U.S. Navy to the sending of battleships to the Royal Navy; it was seen as a threat to the Mahanian strategic theory of conserving a single main battle fleet for a decisive battle. Prolonged negotiation between the navies produced a consensus that a division of U.S. battleships should be sent and that they should be coal-burning rather than oil-fired, to take advantage of Britain's huge coal resources.

Meanwhile, USS *Texas*, in the New York Navy Yard, sent a 5-inch-gun crew to join a newly armed merchantman, *Mongolia*, for its next journey across the Atlantic. On 17 April 1917, *Mongolia* encountered a surfaced U-boat; the *Texas* gun crew fired what was the first U.S. shot in the war. This gave the gun crew's members bragging rights, which they shared with their shipmates when they returned to their ship.

With the end of the scheduled overhaul, USS *Texas* left the New York Navy Yard by way of the East River and the Long Island Sound. Rounding Block Island she ran onto a shelving beach off the northern end of the island after misjudging the turn into the Long Island Sound, with such force that half the length of her hull rested on the sand. The forward double bottoms and four watertight compartments were flooded. The ship was heavily laden with ammunition, coal, and supplies, which had to be offloaded to lighten the ship. After three days and nights of unloading over 4,000 tons of weight and moving both eight-ton anchors to the stern, a small fleet of tugboats was able to pull USS *Texas* free of the sand and of a house-sized rock that had been holding her fast. She was towed back to the dry-dock for repairs that took from 4 October until 5 December 1917. Besides repairing the outer bottom from the bow to amidships, the navy yard removed three of the 5-inch guns: one each from the port and starboard midships battery and the tail stinger.

While the USS *Texas* was being repaired, USS *New York* (with ten 14-inch guns), *Wyoming* (with twelve 12-inch guns), *Florida* (with ten 12-inch guns) and *Delaware* (with ten 12-inch guns)—the ships of Battleship Division 9—all sailed on 25 November to Great Britain to join the Grand Fleet. They ships arrived on 7 December at Scapa Flow in the Orkney Islands of Scotland, the base from which of the Royal Navy's Grand Fleet blockaded the German High Seas Fleet and the German economy.

SCAPA FLOW

The U.S. battleships at Scapa Flow were under the command of Admiral Hugh Rodman, who sailed in USS *New York*. Admiral Rodman had been directed by Admiral William Benson, Chief of Naval Operations in Washington, DC, to place Battleship Division 9 under the operational control of Admiral David Beatty, commander-in-chief of the Grand Fleet. Admiral Rodman also reported to Admiral Sims, in London, and bore command responsibility for the U.S. Navy in the war zone.

Admiral Rodman began the task of integrating his battleships with those of the Grand Fleet, which had been operating on a war footing for three years. This involved becoming experienced with Royal Navy signals, codes, and wireless and telegraph procedures, as well as British tactical maneuvers. This was a huge task but was completed successfully, and Battleship Division 9 became the Sixth Battle Squadron of the Grand Fleet. Recognizing the firepower of U.S. battleships, Admiral Beatty placed the Sixth Battle Squadron, together with the 15-inch-gun Fifth Battle Squadron of the Royal Navy, at the rear of the fleet when sailing eastward and in the van steaming westward. This structure meant that the most heavily armed ships would always be at the head of the fleet if it met the enemy.

The absence of USS *Texas* created scheduling difficulties at Scapa Flow with regard to regular maintenance. All battleships at Scapa Flow were required to be able to get to sea with four hours' notice, sometimes an hour and a half. This requirement drove a need for regular maintenance and refit. When on one occasion USS *New York* was withdrawn from the battle line, there was no other 14-inch-gun ship available to take her place. Both Rodman and Sims pressed Washington for the speedy repair of USS *Texas* and return to rejoin the division in Scapa Flow.

Texas, following her repairs, exercised off Long Island to ensure that her seaworthiness had not been compromised. During a heavy squall she lost three men overboard and could rescue only one. Additionally, it was found that in heavy weather the two forward 5-inch guns, casemates in the wardroom, let in so much seawater as to be unworkable. Back in New York Navy Yard these two guns were removed and the ports plated over.

On 30 January USS *Texas* sailed for Scapa Flow, arriving on 11 February. Met by a Royal Navy cruiser and two destroyers to act as her escort and guide she entered from the Atlantic side the Pentland Firth, which separates the Orkney Islands from Scotland. She then turned north to pass through the Sound of Hoxa to enter the massive anchorage of Scapa Flow and join Division 9.

Captain Victor Blue, commanding officer of USS *Texas*, may have been uneasy at having to sail his ship through the treacherous Pentland Firth and into Scapa Flow, having been on the bridge when she ran aground at the eastern entrance of Long Island Sound. The Pentland Firth opened at the western end to the Atlantic and to the east on the North Sea. This firth (estuary) produced some of the fastest tides in the world, as much as 16 knots, along with four tidal races that could generate whirlpools and very steep waves. The strength of the tidal forces could move a large ship ten degrees off her course.

Safely through the firth, however, USS *Texas* anchored at "Scapa" and was joined by a collier. The next morning paravanes and other minesweeping gear were delivered and installed, as well as a winch for a kite balloon and its electrical connections. A signals officer from the fleet brought lead-bound signal and code books, accompanied by two Royal Navy chief yeomen of signals who were to stay on board until the ship's signal crew was familiar with these new flag and wireless systems.

After a few days to clean the ship and repair the damage from storms encountered crossing the Atlantic, she sailed with the Sixth Battle Squadron and the Grand Fleet to support a convoy of merchant ships to Scandinavia. Room 40 in London had indicated that German battle cruisers were under way and heading north, possibly to intercept the Scandinavian convoy. This sortie, in which the Grand Fleet experienced storms and heavy seas, gave *Texas* ready experience of life at war in the North Sea, as well as of the frustrations of trying to catch the German fleet. The German battle cruisers had returned to their harbor, without locating the convoy. For her part, USS *Texas* received much praise for having been ready to take part in a complex operation within four days of arriving at Scapa Flow.

The USS *Texas*, with her ten 14-inch guns, gave Admiral Rodman the fire-control capability he wanted. The 14-inch guns of *New York* and *Texas*, 20 in all, had the same muzzle velocities and maximum ranges, 23,000 yards, which allowed the two ships to concentrate their fire on one enemy ship in a fleet-to-fleet battle. This was indeed the fire-control doctrine of the Grand Fleet. Homogeneity of gun calibre and muzzle velocity were important for spotting the fall of shot, as the shell splashes would be similar. In addition, fire-control data could be shared between the paired firing ships. The battle instructions of the Grand Fleet were that fire was to be opened at maximum range and that shooting was to cease at 16,000 yards because of the threat from torpedoes.

As *Texas* settled into the fleet, her officers and crew received a terrific shock: the realization that notwithstanding her excellence in peacetime gunnery practice she was well short of the standards of naval battle. Peacetime practice in familiar waters, with established and known distances and no time pressure, did not represent battle experience. Her first gunnery practice was conducted on Scapa Flow's range in rough seas; target range was unknown and had to be determined quickly as the target's course changed. The target-towing ship, the fast Manx steamer *King Orry*, was very experienced at making target shooting realistic and difficult.

This realistic target practice was very different from the target shooting back home, where she had won a pennant for excellence in gunnery. Now the ammunition had to be handled as the ship powered through the swells and waves of the Pentland Firth. The men in the shell rooms had to plug in the padeye to the base of each shell, stored nose down in its rack. Then they had to steer the overhead hoist along the trackway so that the tackle could be lowered and attached to the padeye. They had to lift the shell, all 1,500 pounds of it, from its storage by pulling on the overhead hoist chains and then hand-manage it along the overhead track out of the shell room into the handling room—all without losing control of the suspended shell as it swayed with the ship's movements. Then the shell would be positioned in the lower projectile hoist and hoisted base-first to the upper handling room for transfer to the upper projectile hoist, which moved it up into the turret at the rear of the 14-inch gun. The upper projectile hoist had a cutout at its rear to allow the shell to tilt onto the transfer tray, to be rolled onto the loading tray for ramming into the breach of the gun.

The powder bags followed a different path from the powder magazine. Powder bags were stored in metal tanks, two bags per tank. Each bag weighed 105 pounds. When removed from the tank, by hand, they were placed in a scuttle and transferred to the handling

(top) Fourteen-inch shell and traveling hoist on overhead rail. (bottom) Storage of 14-inch shells, nose down, plus shell hoist, lifting chains, and overhead rail. (Judi Burr)

(counterwise) Central shell and powder hoist mechanism. Closeup of central shell hoist. Powder scuttle on deck of 14-inch-gun house through which powder bags are hand-passed to the gun crew. (Judi Burr)

powder handlers who placed the powder bags on the loading tray to follow the shell into the gun breach. The powder handlers in the gun pits for the superfiring turrets, numbers two and four, then had to lie down on the sloping floor of the gun pit, the breach and lower section of the gun barrel above them. When the muzzle of the barrel was raised to fire, the breach and the lower section of the barrel descended into the gun pit and then recoiled when fired. The gun-pit powder handlers had to move up and down the gun-pit slope, both to move the bags to the gun-loading area and to avoid being crushed by the gun breach. (These men were called "powder monkeys" by the rest of the crew, a reference to how quickly they had to move. The term originated in the days of sail, for the young boys who had to carry bags of gunpowder from below-deck magazines to the gun decks.)

room through the rotating action of the scuttle. In the handling room they were hand transferred from the scuttle to the powder hoist, which lifted the powder bags to the powder flat. From this location, the powder bags were moved by a further hoist to the powder transfer room, where they were placed in a chute and moved through a door into the gun pit. Powder handlers in the gun pit then carried the powder bags up the slope of the gun pit and passed them to additional

(left) Powder room, showing powder canister and storage rack. (right) Powder room scuttle. (Judi Burr)

It took a good deal of practice for the 70 men in a gun turret to hoist a shell and its powder bags, load, and fire the guns in minimum time. Meanwhile their comrades in the spotting top and plotting room identified the target, established gun elevation, bearing, and deflection, and sent the data to dials at the stations of two "pointers" in the front of the turret, who respectively elevated the gun and trained the turret to match the dials, at which point the gunnery officer could fire the guns.

Admiral Rodman later commented of USS *Texas*, "In spite of her four years' commission, that she has now the gunnery trophy, and was flying the efficiency pennant, she was not ready to fire under war conditions." However, his remark at the time was more caustic: "A mud scow should shoot better than the *Texas* did! Will you tell me what the British Commander in Chief must think of our trophy ship?" Comments like this upset the *Texas* crew and apparently circulated throughout the force—but relief was at hand. At an intership soccer match played on the miserable treeless and windswept island of Flotta inside Scapa Flow, where the canteen offered only a cup of tea. A crew member from HMS *Warspite* among the spectators made a disparaging remark about *Texas*' gunnery. The energetic fight it provoked between the two crews restored morale, and subsequently USS *Texas* gunnery improved.

One gunnery problem, however, plagued all of Admiral Rodman's battleships, the excessive dispersion of shell impacts, measured by "spread." The spread was the distance between the impact point of the shell that fell the farthest short of the target and of the one that, passing over the target, struck farthest beyond it. The target would be somewhere between the "short" and the "over." To increase the likelihood of hitting the target the shot needed to fall in as small a pattern as possible, grouped around, ideally on, the target. Early gunnery practice with full-caliber firing with the Grand Fleet resulted in a spread of shot of 757 yards. Grand Fleet battleship spread was 400 yards. As gunnery practice took place for the U.S. battleships the spread reduced until it matched that of the Grand Fleet.

The Sixth Battle Squadron was soon charged with independent operations. On 8 March 1918, the squadron sailed with an antisubmarine screen of destroyers to cover another Scandinavian convoy, this one sailing for Stavanger, Norway. The squadron and convoy parted company just outside Stavanger. The battleships and screen stayed at sea to pick up a returning convoy the next morning. However, before the squadron could reach the rendezvous it ran into a thick fog bank, and there were a number of near collisions. The screening force, however, located the convoy, and the battleships took up their supporting positions the following morning. The force sighted two periscopes and was advised by wireless from Room 40 that its direction-finding section had detected submarine activity in the area. Warned by this intelligence from Room 40, the squadron, the screening destroyers, and the convoy all reached their destinations without harm.

On 8 April 1918, the ships of the Grand Fleet left Scapa Flow for a new base at Rosyth located on the Firth of Forth. USS *Texas* and the rest of her squadron anchored off Hound Point, on the seaward side of the Forth Bridge. Around the ship were the green hills and trees of the Scottish regions of Fife and Lothian, vastly different from the bare, windswept hills that surrounded Scapa Flow. Also, on the southern bank was Edinburgh, spreading over three hills. With access to civilization but with shore leave limited to afternoons, the officers and men of the squadron decided to arrange a theatrical cabaret show. Acquiring boatloads of lumber from ashore, they built a stage beside the superfiring number-four turret, extending over the side. The ship's sailmakers and painters arranged curtains, backdrops, and wing assemblies; the electricians constructed footlights and spotlights. The show was put on by the sailors of the squadron and invites went out to senior officers on other ships within the division and those of the Grand Fleet. The show was a great success and left morale high.

The surrounding communities made available sporting grounds that quickly became baseball fields. The *Texas* team defeated one from *Delaware*, and that initiated competition with the baseball teams of other battleships of the squadron. The *Texas* team took on two U.S. Army teams and won, but then it came up against the U.S. Navy London office, whose team included five professional players, including pitcher Herb Pennock and infielder Mike McNally, both of the Boston Red Sox. The *Texas* team suffered a defeat. Admiral Rodman, knowing the importance of teamwork and morale (and that the British didn't play the game), declared *Texas* the baseball champion of the entire Grand Fleet, with eight wins and just one loss.

During the stay in the Firth of Forth, a kite balloon was taken aboard and sent aloft with two observers in

Antiaircraft gun crew looking for submarines, spring 1918. (Texas Parks & Wildlife Department)

the basket, where in action they would spot the fall of the shot and search the horizon for enemy ships. The Grand Fleet, in addition to supporting convoys to Scandinavia, would make sweeps through the North Sea to entice the German fleet out to fight, sometimes returning to Scapa Flow to take advantage of its long-range gunnery practice areas.

On 30 June 1918, the Sixth Battle Squadron sailed from Scapa Flow to support an ongoing operation to lay a mine barrier across the North Sea between the Orkney Islands and the Udsire Light off the Norwegian coast. This barrier was designed to prevent U-boats from breaking into the Atlantic. The squadron supported Mine Squadron 1 of the Atlantic Fleet, comprising the converted cruiser USS *San Francisco* and the converted liners *Canonicus*, *Canandaigua*, and *Housatonic*. By 26 October 1918, the mine barrier was 230 miles long and between 15 and 35 miles wide. The minefield had three layers, the first covering the surface, the second between 90 and 160 feet deep, and the third between 160 and 240 feet.

The Sixth Battle Squadron sighted submarine periscopes to the south of the minelayers. All of its ships and the accompanying destroyers opened fire, the destroyers dropping depth charges as well. Again, Room 40 wireless-direction intercepted U-boat radio transmissions from the area. On its return to Scapa Flow, the squadron linked up with a Scandinavian convoy and covered it until nightfall.

To mark the Fourth of July the squadron was allowed several days' respite from drills and exercises. It shifted its anchorage to the north shore of Scapa Flow, close to the town of Kirkwall and its Temperance Hotel, which served alcohol.

On 20 October USS *Texas* sailed to Newcastle upon Tyne for dry-docking at nearby Jarrow Slake so that her hull could be cleaned and its antifouling paint renewed. Her boilers were overhauled, and a new, enclosed bridge structure was installed to protect bridge watch standers from winter storms.

In a taste of things to come, a wooden ramp was built and fitted on top of turret two to carry and launch an aircraft. One of the reasons why the Grand Fleet believed it had been unable to catch the German fleet at sea was the German navy's zeppelin scouting force. This zeppelin capability potentially gave it sufficient warning of the approach of the British to avoid them and return to harbor. The Grand Fleet had carried seaplanes on its sweeps into the North Sea, but a ship had to stop and lower the seaplane onto the sea so it could take off, and again to recover it. To overcome this difficulty some ships of the Grand Fleet were equipped with turret-mounted wooden ramps and Sopwith Pup aircraft (which, not being seaplanes, returned to land bases). In June 1917, Squadron-Commander F. Rutland, RN, flew a Sopwith Pup off a twenty-foot-long wooden ramp on the forward turret of HMS *Yarmouth*, a light cruiser. Taking a fighter aircraft to sea enabled the Navy to attack zeppelins without having to stop a ship first. On 21 April 1918, *Yarmouth*, on a sweep off the Jutland coast, was followed by a zeppelin, *L 23*. Flight Sub-Lieutenant B. Smart took off in the ship's Sopwith Pup, climbed to 7,000 feet, and shot down *L 23*, in the first sea-based fighter interception of an enemy aircraft.

Newcastle upon Tyne was not as friendly to the *Texas* crew as Scotland had been. On every shore leave the men got into fights with stevedores and sailors, but at least this gave them the opportunity to take out on unfriendly Tynesiders their frustration at having no chance to fight the German fleet. *Texas* rejoined the fleet from Newcastle on 5 November 1918 and shared in the disgust pervading the fleet at the news that German sailors had mutinied, refusing orders to sail out to battle the Grand Fleet.

SURRENDER OF HIGH SEAS FLEET

The Grand Fleet, with the American dreadnoughts of the Sixth Battle Squadron, did finally meet the High Seas Fleet, on 21 November 1918, but not in battle. Following the signing of the Armistice on 11 November, it was agreed by the allies that the German fleet, once surrendered, would be interned at Scapa Flow while the terms of peace between the allies and the Central Powers of Germany and Austria were decided at Versailles.

USS *Texas* was under way at 3:35 a.m. on 21 November to participate in Operation ZZ, the surrender of the High Seas Fleet to the Grand Fleet. The Sixth Battle Squadron's flagship, USS *New York*, flying the flag of Vice Admiral Sims, representing Admiral Benson, was in the lead, followed immediately by USS *Texas* and thereafter *Arkansas* (which had replaced *Delaware*), *Florida*, and *Wyoming*. At 6:18 a.m. the squadron passed the Isle of May, which marks the mouth of the Firth of Forth, and headed due east.

At 8:45 a.m. the Grand Fleet sighted the cruiser HMS *Cardiff*, which Admiral Beatty had charged with meeting the High Seas Fleet, under the command of Admiral Ludwig von Reuter, just off the German coast and then leading it north to the Firth of Forth to surrender. When the German ships arrived off the firth and turned west to enter it, the Grand Fleet changed course to parallel them.

The German dreadnought battleships and battle cruisers had made their longest voyage in the North Sea during the 1914–18 naval war—to surrender themselves. This fabled High Seas Fleet—battle cruisers *Seydlitz*, *Derfflinger*, *Von der Tann*, *Hindenburg*, and *Moltke*, and battleships *Friedrich der Grosse*, *Albert*, *Kaiser*, *Kronprinz Wilhelm*, *Kaiserin*, *Bayern*, *Markgraf*, *Prinz Regent Luitpold*, and *Grosser Kürfurstk*—was met by 42 dreadnought battleships and battle cruisers of the Grand Fleet, battle flags streaming from their mastheads, arranged in two columns six miles apart. Each column was more than ten miles long. The Sixth Battle Squadron, with USS *Texas*, was in the middle of the northern column.

The German battleship *König* arrived later as a result of shipyard delays in repairing equipment.

Her sailors looked on the ships of the High Seas Fleet with very mixed emotions. They had spent months training for battle and an opportunity to test their skills against the world's second-largest navy, and now before their eyes steamed a line of modern, undamaged dreadnoughts that, to all appearances, could

Surrendered German battle cruiser, November 1918. (Texas Parks & Wildlife Department)

USS *Texas*' band ashore in Scotland, September 1918, the Firth of Forth bridge in background. (Texas Parks & Wildlife Department)

be ready for battle within 24 hours. However, these enemy ships were in fact being herded into captivity under the watchful eyes of the largest, best armed, best trained, and most battle-ready fleet of dreadnoughts ever assembled.

The High Seas Fleet, led by *Cardiff*, a light cruiser, sailed into the Firth of Forth between the two columns

Postwar cleanup, feeding surplus items into a furnace, late 1918. (NARA)

of their adversaries, three miles away on each beam. The Grand Fleet was prepared for battle, powder and shells in their loading trays ready to be rammed, directors and armored conning towers trained on German ships, continuously calculating range and deflection. The High Seas Fleet anchored off Still Point, Inchkeith, for the night. USS *Texas* and the rest of the Sixth Battle Squadron returned to their anchorage in the firth at 2:18 p.m.

Admiral Beatty signaled Admiral Reuter, "The German flag will be hauled down at sunset and will not be raised again without permission."

The war ended, and the German fleet safely under the guns of the Grand Fleet, life could start returning to peacetime routines. The Grand Fleet's Fourth Battle Squadron (HMS *Hercules*, *Colossus*, *Neptune*, and *St. Vincent*, under Admiral Montague Browning, who had been commander-in-chief of the North American and West Indies Station until the previous February), helped the American crews mark Thanksgiving 1918 by hosting celebratory lunches on board, at anchor in the firth.

USS *Texas* now coaled for the nineteenth and last time as part of the Grand Fleet—having loaded 16,000 tons of coal there. In preparation for leaving, the Grand Fleet code and signal books were returned and a collection taken up among the crew for a "homeward-bound" pennant to be made ashore to fly from the mainmast as the ship sailed.

HOMEWARD BOUND

On 1 December 1918, the Sixth Battle Squadron left the firth, escorted by Admiral Beatty and the Fifth Battle Squadron as far as May Island. Goodwill messages reverberated between the squadron and the Grand Fleet, ships' bands played, and ships' sirens blew, all marking how well the Sixth Battle Squadron and the Grand Fleet had worked together.

The squadron was sailing to meet President Woodrow Wilson, who was enroute from Washington, DC.

The squadron anchored in Portland on the English south coast, where it joined with USS *Utah*, *Oklahoma*, and *Arizona* on 4 December 1918. The combined force sailed on the 12th, joined with USS *George Washington* (a naval transport and ex-German liner

Victory fleet in the Hudson River. USS *New York* is in the foreground & USS *Texas* in the background. (NARA)

carrying President Wilson, his wife, and his staff for the Paris Peace conference), and the battleship USS *Pennsylvania*, which had escorted the president across the Atlantic. USS *George Washington* and the nine battleships docked at Brest, France, on 13 December, and President Wilson and his party took a train to Paris.

While the battleships were docked, U.S. Army officers came aboard as passengers for the return voyage to the United States. *Texas* also embarked three aircraft for trials in home waters. At 2 p.m. on the 14th the ship and her fellow battleships departed Brest for their home port, New York.

The group steamed 4,140 miles across the Atlantic and reached New York City in time for Christmas Day 1918. However, Secretary of the Navy Josephus Daniels prevented the battleships from entering until 26 December, so that he could attend the squadron's entry into the harbor and the celebrations of their return from the war zone.

While the officers and men of USS *Texas* reacquainted themselves with New York and life in a peacetime

navy, a diplomatic "naval battle" was emerging in Paris. During the 1919 Paris Peace Talks, the heads of the U.S. Navy and Royal Navy—Admiral William Benson, Chief of Naval Operations, and Admiral Rosslyn Wemyss, First Sea Lord—had to come to grips with the disposition of the German High Seas Fleet. Additionally, the growth and building plans of the U.S. Navy to achieve President Wilson's wish for "a navy second to none" were at odds with the Admiralty's requirement for naval preeminence to safeguard the empire, as the Royal Navy had done for hundreds of years.

The disposition of the surrendered High Seas Fleet was removed from consideration in Paris when the ships, interned in Scapa Flow, scuttled themselves on 21 June 1919. The "naval battle of Paris" thereafter focused on the respective sizes of the U.S. Navy and Royal Navy and the competitive naval building that might result, like the naval race between Germany and England that had been a major cause of World War I. Diplomats took up the discussion from the admirals,

Above. — The superdreadnoughts in single file steaming past Miss Liberty on their way to anchorage up the Hudson, as seen from an airplane. *Photo by Levick.*

Left. — Admiral William T. Mayo, whose blue flag flies from the Pennsylvania, flagship of the mighty fleet. *Tribune Photo*

Our Overseas Battle Fleet
drops anchor in the Hudson

The Atlantic battleship fleet is home again. Here are the twelve great first line fighting ships that are paying Father Knickerbocker a two weeks' visit. Over a hundred of Uncle Sam's grim sea warriors gray the North River, while their 30,000 sailormen are given the freedom of the city in a royal welcome home.

The Battleship ARKANSAS.

The Battleship NEW YORK, flagship of Rear Admiral A. Rodman.

The Battleship FLORIDA.

The bargeload of gobs come ashore from the Pennsylvania.

The Battleship TEXAS.

The Battleship OKLAHOMA.

The Battleship DELAWARE.

The Battleship UTAH, flagship of Rear Admiral E. W. Eberle.

The Battleship NEVADA.

The Battleship PENNSYLVANIA, flagship of Admiral Mayo.

The Battleship WYOMING, flagship of Rear Admiral R. E. Coontz.

The Battleship NORTH DAKOTA.

The Battleship Mississippi leading the fleet into the harbor, as photographed from an airplane. Note the airplanes atop the forward and aft turrets. *Photo by Levick.*

Parade of American naval might: battleships of the Atlantic Fleet entering New York Harbor, April 1919. (Library of Congress) and on 10 April, Col. Edward M. House, on behalf of President Wilson, and Lord Robert Cecil, on behalf of David Lloyd George, the prime minister of the United Kingdom, reached an understanding on these issues, the urgency of which lessened as the plans for a League of Nations and the terms of the peace with Germany and Austria were negotiated. However, the "naval battle" would reemerge in 1921 and have major and ongoing impact on USS *Texas*.

On 31 December 1918, Captain Nathan Twining took command of the USS *Texas* in New York. After a month in the navy yard the ship got under way for Guantanamo Bay, stopping for three days in Hampton Roads with the Atlantic Fleet. Guantanamo Bay meant more drills and exercises. The most important exercise occurred on 9 March 1919, the launching of a Sopwith Camel aircraft from the 1918 Newcastle-built platform over number-two turret of USS *Texas*. The Camel was piloted by Lt. Commander Edward McDonnell, who flew the aircraft off the 20-foot platform while the ship was at anchor. The Camel was a very light aircraft and had performed this exercise many times before on Royal Navy ships; it landed at the Guantanamo Bay base, as it was not capable of landing on the ship or on the water. The aircraft also participated in gunnery exercises, spotting the fall of shot of the 14-inch guns. *Texas* was the first U.S. battleship to launch an aircraft, and the capabilities that were then seen to be possible would be significantly used in later years.

In April 1919, the Atlantic Fleet returned to New York to prepare for participation in a transatlantic crossing by U.S. Navy Curtis aircraft. These four seaplanes departed from the naval air station at Rockway, New York, on 8 May 1919. Aerial navigation instruments for flying the distance from New York to Lisbon, Portugal, were very limited, and the seaplanes would have no reference points once over the sea. Accordingly, the U.S. Navy stationed ships, one of them USS *Texas*, every fifty miles across the Atlantic to support the seaplanes by radio with navigation and weather data. Only one seaplane out of the four reached Lisbon.

On 4 June, the ship took on 300 new Marine recruits and 200 new crew members at Hampton Roads, the body of water before the Chesapeake Bay, and the site of the famous battle between USS *Monitor* and CSS *Virginia*. This allowed USS *Texas* to pay off the wartime crew members and reserve officers in New York starting on 19 June.

USS *Texas*' Sopwith Camel. (Judi Burr)

The latest thing in whizz buggies: a Sopwith Camel on top of a USS *Texas* gun turret. (Texas Parks & Wildlife Department)

First flight of an airplane off number-two gun turret, flown by Lieutenant Commander McDonnell, Guantanamo Bay, 10 March 1919. Note gun turret pointing out to port for the takeoff. (Texas Parks & Wildlife Department)

No. 1 airplane being readied for flight on top of a *Texas* gun turret, 10 March 1919. (Texas Parks & Wildlife Department)

USS *Texas* in upper east chamber of Gatun Lock during her passage to the Pacific, 25 July 1919. (NARA)

TO THE PACIFIC

With the end of World War I the U.S. Navy began to review its strategy and recognized that it had very limited capability on the West Coast. The 28 June 1919 Paris Peace Conference had given Japan a mandate to control the Pacific islands of the Marshalls, Marianas, and Carolines. These islands, previously governed by Germany, had been invaded and taken by the Japanese navy in October 1914. This meant that Japan's sphere of influence and control now extended eastward across the Pacific and potentially threatened American communications with the Philippines.

President Wilson, who needed the support of his West Coast Democrats to pass the League of Nations treaty, ordered that seven battleships—USS *Texas, New York, New Mexico, Idaho, Mississippi, Wyoming,* and *Arkansas*—be sent to the West Coast, to be stationed at San Pedro, near Los Angeles. These ships transited the Panama Canal in July 1919 and were met at San Diego by Secretary Daniels, who accepted a 19-gun salute. The fleet showed the flag from San Diego to Seattle, where their visit coincided with a speech on the League of Nations by President Wilson. On 16 January 1920, USS *Texas* arrived at San Pedro, which now became the permanent base for the U.S. Pacific Fleet.

Long overdue for maintenance, USS *Texas* arrived at Puget Sound on 15 April 1920 and entered the navy yard at Bremerton, Washington, for a six-month overhaul. During this period her engines, boilers, pumps, and dynamos were all rebuilt, broadside directors were installed to govern the 5-inch guns, and a new plotting room and radio installation were fitted. The

USS *Texas* at anchor, Los Angeles, 1919. (Library of Congress)

masts were given a new torpedo-defense station, the searchlight platforms were raised, and new antiaircraft guns installed. While the technical and building work progressed the crew were charged with removing all the paint down to the bare metal and then applying new coats to the hull above and below the waterline. Decks both internal and external were replaced where worn, and weather decks were recaulked where necessary.

USS *Texas* sailed from Bremerton on 1 October and rejoined the Pacific Fleet in San Pedro. She carried on her deck seven cars and twenty-one motorbikes. It was rumored that several members of the crew had stowed their wives on board as well. Back with the fleet, she then sailed to San Francisco before leaving on 5 January 1921 and joined the Atlantic Fleet off Balboa, Panama, on 17 January. The officers and crew then enjoyed five days of leave before sailing for Valparaiso, Chile, for

fleet exercises, returning for more leave at Balboa on 14 February.

Since the overhaul in Bremerton the crew had begun to feel that USS *Texas* was now an old ship, a dirty coal-burner, and did not compare with the new battleships like USS *New Mexico*, with turboelectric drive, turbine propulsion, and triple-gun turrets. Crew performance and morale began to suffer. However, a new executive officer, who had been a junior officer on board USS *Texas* at her commissioning and therefore remembered how smart and efficient she had been seven years before, came aboard and began the task of reinvigorating both officers and crew.

During her time in the Pacific Fleet the "naval battle of Paris" between the U.S. Navy and the Royal Navy was revived by the new president, Warren Harding. The Navy began to be concerned with the implications

Crew training with the range finder. (Texas Parks & Wildlife Department)

of the Anglo-Japanese naval alliance following the award of Pacific islands to Japan. Additionally, the disparity in size of the dreadnought fleets of the U.S. and Royal Navy made it imperative to build all the ships projected by the 1916 and 1918 programs to achieve parity with the Royal Navy. The mood in the American public and in Congress, however, had begun to mellow since the end of the war. President Harding's new secretary of state, Charles Hughes, invited the major naval powers to a conference in Washington, DC, during November 1921, to discuss both naval arms control and security issues in the Pacific. At this conference Hughes took all the delegates by surprise with a detailed plan to halt new naval shipbuilding and to scrap a large number of existing ships, leaving the United States, Great Britain, and Japan with capital ships in the ratio of 5:5:3. There would then be a ten-year pause in capital-ship building to maintain the ratio and avoid a new naval race.

The emergence of naval aviation was recognized by a tonnage limit for aircraft carriers, at the level of 135,000 tons for

USS *Texas* in dry-dock for hull cleaning and painting, fall 1919, Bremerton. (Texas Parks & Wildlife Department)

the United States and for Great Britain, 81,000 tons for Japan, and 60,000 tons each for France and Italy.

An important addition to the conference was an agreement between the United States, Great Britain, Japan, and France to respect the other parties' possessions. By this means the Anglo-Japanese naval alliance was canceled, to the relief of the U.S. Navy.

The Americans had to scrap eleven battleships authorized for the next several years but retained eighteen. With the full implementation of the agreement this number would be reduced to fifteen,

the same number as the Royal Navy. Japan was allowed to retain nine battleships. The Washington Naval Conference and agreement meant for USS *Texas* a clear future for the next decade, as one of the eighteen battleships allowed.

Texas continued to operate on the West Coast until January 1924, when she transited the Panama Canal to the Caribbean and Atlantic to take aboard Naval Academy midshipmen for their summer cruise, which included visits to England, France, Holland, Gibraltar, and the Azores.

Fourteen-inch gun being replaced at Bremerton Naval Yard, mid-1920. (Texas Parks & Wildlife Department)

Fourteen-inch gun nearly in place. Bremerton Naval Yard, mid-1920. (Texas Parks & Wildlife Department)

Fourteen-inch gun being delivered to USS *Texas* at Bremerton Navy Yard. (Texas Parks & Wildlife Department)

USS *Texas* passing through the Panama Canal. (U.S. Naval Institute photo archive)

Normal peacetime drills and exercises occupied USS *Texas* until 19 November 1924, when she left Hampton Roads for the waters off the Virginia Capes to test the armor of BB-47, one of the battleships to be scrapped under the Washington conference. BB-47, which was to have been USS *Washington*, had been launched on 1 September 1921; all work had been stopped on 8 February 1922, two days after the signing of the Washington Naval Agreement. BB-47 was 76 percent complete, her armor in place, and the Navy wanted to test her armor arrangements rather than just scrap her.

Towed to the site, BB-47 was first hit by two 400-pound torpedoes. Then three one-tonne bombs were dropped, meant to explode near her hull but not on board. These bombs produced a list of three degrees.

Then a single charge of 400 pounds of TNT was detonated on board, with little visible effect. Next, fourteen 14-inch shells were dropped by aircraft from 4,000 feet; only one penetrated her armor deck.

BB-47 continued to float, even through a passing storm. On 25 November, USS *Texas* and *New York* were positioned to fire. After a full ten-gun salvo by *Texas*, BB-47 remained afloat, which allowed observers to board BB-47 and examine and photograph the damage. After they left, a further ten-gun salvo was fired, and BB-47 listed and then started to settle by the bow. After a while the stern lifted, and BB-47 sank. It is historically ironic that USS *Texas*, built to battle enemy dreadnoughts, sank only one dreadnought, and that one was unarmed and originally intended for the U.S. Navy.

Sailors sleeping in hammocks, early 1920s. (Texas Parks & Wildlife Department)

MODERNIZATION

Norfolk Naval Shipyard, Portsmouth, VA, USS *Texas* and USS *North Carolina*, 1 April 1925. (NARA)

The USS *Texas* returned to Hampton Roads and on 31 July 1925 entered the Norfolk Navy Yard (formally the Norfolk Naval Shipyard) to undergo modernization. This process took 16 months and from it a drastically changed USS *Texas* was to emerge.

The modernization program had to comply with the Washington Naval Treaty, which limited the increase in displacement to 3,000 tons, within which improvements to a ship's "passive" defenses against bombs, plunging shells, and torpedoes could be made. Accordingly, the hull was modified by the addition of antitorpedo bulges from just forward of the forward gun turret to just aft of the number-five turret. These bulges increased the beam of the ship from just over 95 feet to 106 feet but still allowed the ship to transit the Panama Canal.

The superstructure was removed, as were the two cage masts, both funnels, and the main deck, to allow access to the armor decks and boiler rooms. The 14 boilers were scrapped in place, one of the four fire rooms was removed, and the remainder were heavily modified to allow six new Bureau Express three-drum oil-fired boilers to be installed, two to a fire room. These new boilers had been originally ordered for the canceled *South Dakota*–class battleships. The space saved by the reduction in fire rooms was used for a new, enlarged plotting room for fire control, electrical switching, internal communications, storerooms, and new internal longitudinal bulkheads. Also, a third bottom was added above the original double bottom.

USS *Texas* in dry-dock at Norfolk Navy Yard, showing scaffolding for construction of hull blisters. (NARA)

(clockwise from above) Refurbished boiler face and controls; boiler face; engine room dials. (Judi Burr)

Port battery 5-inch gun. (Judi Burr)

Three Vought Corsair aircraft stored on the catapult on top of number-three gun turret. (Texas Parks & Wildlife Department)

The change from coal to oil meant a major improvement in the ship's cleanliness, by eliminating the clouds of coal dust that affected both the ship and crew. The size of the crew was reduced by the elimination of coal handlers, as was the number of funnels, to just one. The most significant change for USS *Texas*, however, was the increase in its endurance under steam. Its range rose from 7,060 miles on coal power to 15,400 miles on fuel oil.

Additional armor plate was fitted to the second and third decks, for a total of 250 tons. Armor was also added to turret roofs. The coal bunkers on the third deck were converted to crew quarters and those below the third deck to fuel oil bunkers.

The 5-inch guns of the secondary battery on the second deck were vulnerable to heavy weather; six of the forwardmost were moved to new positions on the main deck on sponsons, which gave them greater fields of fire. The two torpedo tubes were removed on each side and their associated internal loading and storage space reconfigured to be used as storerooms and a magazine for antiaircraft guns.

Above the main deck, two tripod masts were installed. The mainmast was moved aft to between the third and fourth gun turrets. The foremast now housed a chart house and a navigation bridge, and on top of the mast was a new fire-control center for spotting and controlling both main and secondary armament. A secondary fire-control center was built into a tower just aft of the funnel.

A catapult was built on top of the number-three turret, with the run of the catapult positioned outside the left barrel to allowing it to be elevated for firing and maintenance. A Vought FU-1 float-equipped biplane was allocated to USS *Texas* for spotting gunfire and for scouting. The aircraft was stored on the catapult when not in use. The ship's cranes were both lengthened and strengthened to handle the increased weight of the aircraft.

When USS *Texas* sailed from Norfolk on 23 November 1926, she was a modern battleship. After extensive shakedown in Guantanamo Bay, *Texas* returned to Norfolk on 14 December for the addition of a flag bridge (over the navigation bridge, for an embarked admiral and his staff) and flag accommodations to her bridge structure. USS *Texas* departed the yard on 5 January 1927 and became the new flagship of the United States Fleet, into which the Navy's operating forces were organized from 1922 to 1945.

Back in service, changes in performance revealed themselves. The blisters made the ship roll and wallow more, to the extent that supplying the main guns with shells from below became unsafe in particular sea conditions. Also, the reciprocating steam engines, which remained, became troublesome. At cruising speed, propeller-shaft vibration was so strong as to cause concerns that the shafts might crack. However, this did not happen, and USS *Texas* steamed on.

(left) Engine piston; (below left) piston head; (below right) engine-revolution counter. (Judi Burr)

FLAGSHIP OF THE UNITED STATES FLEET

Under the command of Adm. Henry Wiley, commander-in-chief of the United States Fleet, USS *Texas* sailed to and through the Panama Canal to lead the Fleet Problem IX strategic exercise. These exercises pitted half of the fleet against the other half in simulated warfare to test strategies and tactics. That year's exercise was the first in which the competing fleets both had aircraft carriers. USS *Lexington* and *Saratoga* had both become operational, and fleet commanders, along with the Naval War College, were anxious to test their capabilities in a fleet structure.

Admiral Joseph M. Reeves, Commander Air Squadrons, convinced Admiral William V. Pratt, commanding the aggressor ("Black") fleet, to detach USS *Saratoga* with a single escort to "attack" the Panama Canal. USS *Saratoga* launched her aircraft and caught the Panama Canal's defenders by surprise. *Saratoga* had avoided the "Blue" (U.S.) fleet and thus demonstrated that aircraft carriers were capable of independent task-force roles. However, it was also shown that aircraft carriers were very vulnerable if found by an opposing warship, as USS *Saratoga* experienced toward the end of the exercise.

USS Texas entering Havana Harbor from Malecon

Vought SBU Corsair aircraft on catapult. (Texas Parks & Wildlife Department)

Crane handling mishap. (Texas Parks & Wildlife Department)

USS *Texas*, carrying President Calvin Coolidge, entering Havana Harbor, January 1928. (Library of Congress)

A powder charge in the catapult fires a Vought O2U Corsair aircraft at 55 mph off USS *Texas* in 1929. (Texas Parks & Wildlife Department)

A view from the stern showing floatplanes on catapult. (Texas Parks & Wildlife Department)

A flyover of USS *Texas* by 180 service aircraft to commemorate the retirement of Admiral Jehu V. Chase, Commander Battle Fleet, San Diego, 14 August 1933. (Texas Parks & Wildlife Department)

Fleet Problem X in 1930, with USS *Texas*, as fleet flagship, again demonstrated the importance of naval aviation to achieving fleet objectives and showed how much it had progressed since *Texas* had launched a Sopwith Camel from a turret in March 1919.

During the 1930s USS *Texas* moved between the East and West Coasts operating as a flagship conducting midshipman training cruises and other training. Of particular note was the training of members of the Fleet Marine Force.

Discussions between the governments of the United States and the United Kingdom had continued after the Washington Naval Conference and had driven further meetings, in Geneva during 1927, that addressed numbers and type of cruisers. The terms of the 1930 London Naval Treaty postponed the replacement of capital ships to 1937, which in turn meant a further reprieve for USS *Texas*, as any battleship built from 1937 onward would not be operational until 1940.

Texas became once again a test bed for new naval technology when on 4 January 1939 she took aboard a prototype radar set. The Radio Corporation of America (RCA) had developed a radar set, designated CXZ, built into a cabinet mounted on wheels to be located on the main deck. A different type of radar, XAF, was tested on board the USS *New York* at the same time; this set had been developed by the Naval Research Laboratory. The CXZ radar gave better definition, but the XAF had a longer range. Following these tests, RCA combined both these features in a new shipborne radar set, CXAM-1. USS *Texas* received one of the early CXAM-1 sets in 1941, with its control room on the port side of the signal bridge.

WORLD WAR II

General Eisenhower speaking to American sailors prior to D-Day, 1944. (U.S. Naval Institute photo archive)

The invasion of Poland by Germany set the world on a course to war. The United States declared itself neutral on 12 September 1939 and commenced naval neutrality patrols in the Atlantic.

USS *Texas* continued her training regime and on 1 February 1941, while in Culebra Bay, Puerto Rico, as flagship for the Caribbean Amphibious Exercise, held a ceremony on the fantail that activated the 1st Marine Division, of which the ship's Marine Detachment would be a part. This division would earn a highly significant place in American and Marine history, by its seizure of Guadalcanal, invasions of Peleliu and Okinawa, and many other instances in its ongoing service to the United States.

USS *Texas* conducted her first neutrality patrol on 23 April 1941. She escorted a convoy to the mid-Atlantic to meet a Royal Navy escort that would convoy the merchant ships on to Great Britain. During another neutrality patrol, in June 1941, a German U-boat, *U-203*, tracked USS *Texas* while radioing U-boat headquarters for permission to attack. Fortunately, permission was denied.

USS *Texas* was berthed in Casco Bay, Portland, Maine, when Pearl Harbor was attacked on 7 December 1941. The ship sailed for Argentia, Canada, on 12 December, the day that the United States declared war against Germany and Italy. The ship streamed paravanes and zigzagged to counter possible submarine torpedo attacks.

In early January 1942, USS *Texas* returned to New York and received 120 new sailors from a naval training station. In addition, the ship took on board two new OS2U Kingfisher floatplanes for scouting and gunfire spotting. On 15 January *Texas* joined Task Force (TF) 15, which comprised an aircraft carrier (USS *Wasp*), a heavy cruiser (USS *Quincy*), two troopships, and Destroyer Division 16. The task force sailed for Iceland, where it arrived on 25 January. The troops were part of an occupation force to prevent Germany from invading the island and using it as a U-boat base.

USS *Texas* returned to Norfolk on 13 March and on 10 April, after replenishing, left Hampton Roads as part of TF 38 for the Panama Canal. *Texas* was escorting a convoy of 17 troopships destined for the Pacific Ocean.

Among the troops was the 1st Marine Division, on the first leg of its journey to Guadalcanal. *Texas* left the convoy at Colon, at the Atlantic end of the Panama Canal, and returned to Norfolk Navy Yard, where she went into dry-dock for regular overhaul on 24 April.

USS *Texas* escorted two more troop convoys across the Atlantic, one to Freetown, Sierra Leone (a British colony in West Africa), and one to the United Kingdom. In both instances the ship's Kingfisher aircraft scouted for submarines. Back in Norfolk from 29 July until 23 October, USS *Texas* engaged in critical exercises in radar control of both surface ships and aircraft. These exercises were conducted using the new SC-1 air-search radar, built by General Electric and installed during this period. Other exercises involved simulated air attacks by bombs and torpedoes, damage control, air defense, and all the ship's armament, including shore bombardment.

OPERATION TORCH

These concentrated and intense exercises were in preparation for what was to be the first U.S.-led military operation against Germany, in conjunction with British forces. The aim was to seize North Africa as a

Commemorative plaque for the founding of the 1st Marine Division on board USS *Texas*. (Judi Burr)

UNITED STATES NAVAL INSTITUTE

springboard for future Allied operations on the European mainland, as well as finally secure the Suez Canal and, collaterally, the Iranian oil fields. A broader consideration was to commit U.S. forces against Germany to ensure the support of the American public for the war in Europe.

Lieutenant General Dwight Eisenhower was selected to command what was to be called Operation Torch. Operation Torch was planned with two broad fronts of attack, the Atlantic coast of Morocco and the Mediterranean coast of French Algeria. The attacks were to be amphibious landings.

The attack on the Atlantic coast, at Casablanca, was spearheaded by the Western Task Force, TF 34. This force comprised 102 ships carrying 35,000 troops, protected by 24 warships, including USS *Texas*. TF 34 sailed from three locations on the East Coast and crossed the Atlantic to North Africa.

On 23 October USS *Texas* sailed from Norfolk and joined a part of the force, Task Group (TG) 34.3. This convoy, one of three, contained 6 troopships with 9,000 Army soldiers, 2 cargo ships carrying 65 tanks, the cruiser USS *Savannah*, and 6 destroyers. This convoy sailed toward Bermuda, with the destroyer screen and the ships' Kingfisher aircraft to protect them from submarines. On 26 October TF 34.3 joined the other two convoys, creating the invasion force, TF 34.

On 7 November TF 34's three groups split again, to conduct the planned landings north and south of Casablanca and at Fedaia, just north of the city. Each task group was to capture a port and related airfield. USS *Texas*, as flagship of the northern group, was assigned to attack and capture Port Lyautey. The northern attack was scheduled for 4:00 a.m. on 8 November. However, moving the troops from the troopships into the landing craft and then maneuvering the landing craft through the high surf to the beaches took far longer than planned, and it was 5:30 a.m. when the first troops actually landed and established a beachhead.

All the Torch beachheads were in French colonies, and France had already been overrun by Germany. Accordingly, there was considerable uncertainty as to whether the French troops would welcome the American troops as allies or resist them as enemies. The hope was that the French forces in Africa (subordinate to not occupied Paris but to Vichy, capital of the "puppet state" comprising the part of France that Germany had left unoccupied) would have a pro-American bias. At Port Lyautey, in fact, it was anticipated that an element of French troops including two division commanders would stage a coup and welcome the invaders. This did not happen, and the Vichy French fired on the American troops.

At 1:43 in the afternoon of the first day a U.S. Army fire-control party called for naval gunfire on a munitions dump inshore from Port Lyautey. *Texas* fired 59 rounds of 14-inch ammunition, the first 14-inch shells fired at an enemy by USS *Texas*. They were fired at a range of eight miles at a target on the "reverse" (far) side of a hill, where it could not be seen from the ship. *Texas* launched her Kingfisher aircraft to direct the fire, since the Army fire-control party didn't have the position to do so themselves. On the afternoon of 10 November, the Kingfisher aircraft located a vehicle convoy on a road leading to Port Lyautey and brought down 64 of its shells of 14-inch, destroying both the convoy and the road and so preventing any more reinforcements from reaching the port.

The Kingfisher performed more adventurous exploits in support of the Army. Lieutenant L. R. Chesley was about to be catapulted from USS *Texas* for an antisubmarine patrol when a report came in that another convoy, of tanks and trucks, was moving toward Port Lyautey from Rabat. The Kingfisher was armed with a depth charge; the aviation crew set the fuse to explode on contact. Catapulted from the ship, the Kingfisher flew to the convoy, released the depth charge from a thousand feet, and scored a direct hit on a tank, causing an explosion that turned over two other tanks as well.

While USS *Texas* oversaw the action at Port Lyautey, her sister ship *New York* was at Safi, the beach south of Casablanca, where her 14-inch guns silenced a number of coastal batteries. The new battleship USS *Massachusetts* was stationed off Casablanca itself to protect U.S. forces from the French battleship *Jean Bart*, in dry-dock but her guns serviceable. In an artillery duel, USS *Massachusetts* hit *Jean Bart* seven times with 16-inch shells, putting her out of action. *Massachusetts* was hit by a 7.64-inch shell fired by the El Hank coastal battery. The shell landed on the deck to port of number-two gun turret, penetrated into a second-deck compartment. and exploded (causing neither casualties nor serious damage).

Operation Torch demonstrated the importance to the Allies of what was later called "sea control." The three convoys of troopships and warships that made up TF 34, had sailed from three separate East Coast ports, joined in midocean, and sailed over 3,000 nautical miles across the Atlantic—the primary arena of the German U-boat offensive against supply convoys to the United Kingdom. TF 34 sailed a more southerly route than the North Atlantic supply convoys did, and it was protected by aircraft from the carrier USS *Ranger* and Kingfishers from the three accompanying battleships, USS *Texas, New York,* and *Massachusetts.* TF 34 reached the North African coast without encountering any German submarines. On 11 November U-boats did reach the invasion force, but by this time the majority of the troops and supplies had been disembarked. U-boats were able to sink four supply ships but at the cost of *U-173.*

Torch was the first step in the joining of U.S. forces with the British Eighth Army, which had been fighting for several years in North Africa from its base in Egypt. The British had to sustain their army and air force by sea from British ports south through the Atlantic, around the Cape of Good Hope, and north through the Indian Ocean and the Red Sea to the Gulf of Suez and Egypt—a distance of 11,000 nautical miles.

(Additionally, the British were able to supply troops from the Commonwealth countries of Australia, New Zealand, and India.)

The German Africa Corps and its Italian elements were, in contrast, supplied directly across the Mediterranean, from the Italian ports of Naples and Taranto to Tunis, a distance of only 300 nautical miles. This supply route, however, was interdicted by Royal Navy submarines from Malta, Royal Air Force (RAF) aircraft both from Malta and Egypt, and surface forces, mainly destroyers and light cruisers, also from Egypt. The U.S. Army Air Forces (USAAF) too bombed ships and German and Italian ports. Nevertheless, the German and Italian armies were kept supplied, if at diminishing volumes.

The Allies' command of the sea in this theater ensured growing capabilities on land and sea and in the air. They were able to push the enemy back and reduce to insignificance the level of supplies it received until both German and Italian troops surrendered, with the fall of Tunis on 13 May 1942.

As for USS *Texas,* she left the North African coast to return to the United States on 15 November 1943, arriving in Norfolk on the 29th. Her next mission was

Quadruple 40-mm Bofors gun. (Judi Burr)

UNITED STATES NAVAL INSTITUTE

to escort a series of supply convoys to British forces at Casablanca, Gibraltar, and other locations.

On 1 June 1943, she entered Boston Navy Yard for an upgrade to her antiaircraft armaments. Ten quadruple 40-millimeter antiaircraft mounts were installed to replace the old 1.1-inch guns, which had proved unreliable and inadequate against modern military aircraft. The ten new mounts presented attacking aircraft with forty barrels firing two-pound shells at a rate of 120 rounds per minute—a far more effective defense against enemy aircraft. In addition, an open space between the signal bridge and the deck of the navigation bridge was enclosed and made into a radar plot by the installation of radars, displays, and communication equipment that had been on the signal bridge.

Next was convoy escort duty across the North Atlantic during winter, a hazardous task even without dealing with U-boat "wolf packs." In January 1944 a storm peeled back a 16-foot section of the port antitorpedo blister. Temporary repairs were made in the River Clyde estuary, on the west coast of Scotland. *Texas* then returned to the Boston Navy Yard escorting a returning convoy. There, in addition to repairs of the antitorpedo blister and repainting of the hull, the 14-inch shell hoists were modified to accommodate new types of armor-piecing and high-capacity rounds. All the old 14-inch shells were removed to make room for the new ammunition. The SG surface-search radar antenna was moved to the foretop, and new high-frequency direction-finding radio equipment was installed. "Huff-Duff," as it was known, determined the direction or bearing from which a radio signal was received and was part of the ship's suite of high technology used to search for submarines. Radar plot was reorganized as the "combat information center," CIC, and equipped with the latest analytical and communication instruments.

On 27 February *Texas* sailed to Casco Bay, Maine, for training in and exercises all the new equipment, in particular the new 40-mm antiaircraft guns. On 31 March USS *Texas* sailed to her home port, New York, and became flagship for Battleship Division 5, under Adm. Carleton Bryant, with USS *Nevada, Arkansas*, and *New York*. On 6 April the division sailed for Great Britain as escorts for a transatlantic supply convoy.

PREPARATION FOR OVERLORD

When USS *Texas* anchored in the Clyde Estuary on the morning of 16 April, only the senior officers were aware that a major event was in store. The crew was given ten days of liberty, light duties, and routine maintenance; the men were about to undergo an intense and extended period of training of all aspects of the ship's operations, from damage control to shore bombardment. The key objectives were to accustom the crew to long periods at General Quarters and to ensure that the arrangements for feeding and resting the crew at battle stations were efficient and effective. Also addressed was an important ingredient of shore bombardment, spotting and communication between the gun director and off-ship spotters. Trials were made with aircraft spotters and then with shore fire-control parties, both naval and Army specialists. Fire control in low visibility using full radar control was also exercised. In the area of damage control the crew was trained to deal with expected forms of damage from mines, bombs, and large-calibre shellfire. Considerable time was taken to study of operational orders and of maps, photographs, and charts of the approach to a target.

As these exercises went on day after day the men became increasingly aware that a significant operation was before them. Their lengthy stay in European waters and the inclusion of Royal Navy ships and aircraft in their exercises reinforced the idea among the crew members that they were going to participate in a major operation against German-occupied France.

On 8 May USS *Texas* moved from the Clyde to Belfast Lough, Northern Ireland, to join TG 129.2, where her fellow task group members were USS *Arkansas*, the heavy cruiser HMS *Glasgow*, and the Free French light cruisers *Georges Leygues* and *Montcalm*. These ships, led by USS *Texas*, would be a bombardment force for their designated beach.

In early May the flight crews of the ship's Kingfisher left the ship to join a new observation squadron, VCS-7, at a Royal Air Force base at Lee-on-Solent, Hampshire. The Kingfishers were removed from the ships of TG 129.2 and placed in storage. The catapult on *Texas'* number-three turret used by the Kingfisher aircraft of USS *Texas*, was removed as unnecessary weight. During the invasion of Sicily in July 1943, the slow Kingfisher aircraft had suffered losses and damage in a hotly contested war zone against German fighter aircraft and antiaircraft fire from the ground.

The planners of the naval component of the invasion, Operation Neptune, under Adm. Bertram Ramsay, RN, were well aware that the waters off what would be the

Normandy invasion beaches would be overrun with vessels, nearly 7,000. There would be 1,213 warships, 4,126 landing craft of multiple types, 726 ancillary craft, and 864 merchant ships in the invasion force. As these vessels would be jockeying for sea space, trying to avoid each other and German shellfire; there would be little room for Kingfisher aircraft to land on the sea near their ships, which themselves would have to maneuver to create the smooth sea surface necessary. For all these reasons the planners decided that the Kingfisher would not be used and that spotting would be done by RAF Spitfires instead.

The Kingfisher aircrews from USS *Texas* and the other bombardment ships were retrained to fly the Spitfire, a fast fighter aircraft designed to dogfight with German fighters and that had already gained fame for its role in the Battle of Britain. VCS-7, commanded by Lieutenant Commander W. Denton Jr., USN, was a composite squadron, with pilots from seven U.S. Navy ships, and six RAF and Fleet Air Arm squadrons. Training lasted from 8 until 28 May, all the pilots qualifying in the Mark V, clipped-wing Spitfire.

While USS *Texas'* former Kingfisher pilots were qualifying with Spitfires and learning how to spot gunfire from a fast-moving aircraft and to dogfight, the rest of the crew continued gunnery and damage-control exercises. USS *Texas* joined with *Nevada* and *Arkansas* in shore-bombardment practice. U.S. Army communication and electronic experts came aboard USS *Texas* to install transmitters and receivers to facilitate communication with Army fire-control parties ashore. Specialized equipment to jam German radar and radio-controlled guided missiles was also installed, in response to the successful use of these new missiles against Allied ships during the recent invasions of Italy.

Belfast Lough also provided the opportunity for weekend liberty, as well as for the privilege on 19 May of meeting and being addressed by General Dwight Eisenhower, Supreme Commander, Allied Expeditionary Force for the planned invasion of France. Assembled on the fantail on a rainy afternoon, the crew heard General Eisenhower note that the ship was named for the state of his birth and welcome them into a great Allied team that had been assembling in Great Britain for 18 months. He then exhorted them to "Knock that damned Hitler out of the war" and assured them that it was only the men that crewed the ships and worked and fired their guns, together with their army and air force

comrades in arms, who would win the war. Generals sitting at their desks, he went on, could only organize and direct, but it was the men of USS *Texas* who fought the war. Following his talk, General Eisenhower toured the ship.

Further bombardment exercises were held in Dundrum Bay, Northern Ireland, once at night using radar to spot and control firing, in support of an infantry landing on a hostile shore. Following these exercises, on 31 May USS *Texas* the sealed envelopes carrying detailed orders for Operation Neptune, the landing of Allied forces on the French beaches of Normandy, were opened and studied. Captain Charles Baker informed his crew that the ship was now was isolated from all external contact in preparation for the real action that they all had been training for, so that no leak to the enemy of their plans could occur.

During the early morning of 3 June 1944, USS *Texas* led the ships of its bombardment force out of Belfast Lough and steamed south through the Irish Sea and St. George's Channel, past the Bristol Channel, and into the Atlantic. They then rounded the westernmost tip of England, Land's End, and entered the English Channel. Their progress was halted when the captain received word at 7:30 a.m. on the 4th that D-Day had been postponed by 24 hours because of bad weather and heavy seas. *Texas* and the ships in company reversed course and steamed back along its earlier track. At 10:00 p.m. they reversed course again so as to be on station off Plymouth by midafternoon on Monday, 5 June. Plymouth—from where Sir Francis Drake had sailed in July 1588 against the Spanish Armada and in September 1620 the *Mayflower* had sailed to establish a settlement in North America—was now one of many English harbors from which an Allied armada was to liberate France and occupied Europe and then invade Germany itself.

USS *Texas* was part of the bombardment force of six battleships: USS *Arkansas*, USS *Nevada*, HMS *Ramillies*, HMS *Rodney*, and HMS *Warspite*. One more battleship, HMS *Nelson*, was held in reserve. Two 15-inch-gun monitors, HMS *Erebus* and *Roberts*, and 23 cruisers completed the bombardment force. Attached were 101 destroyers, there to support the actual landings and protect them from German naval forces.

D-DAY

On 6 June General Eisenhower would deliver a radio address on 6 June to all the soldiers, sailors, and airmen under his command, ending, "We will accept nothing less than full victory!"

Plymouth Harbor was full with hundreds of ships of all types, many flying barrage balloons, so the men of USS *Texas* were well aware they were part of a major and historic operation. This impression was confirmed when just before 11:00 p.m. on 5 June General Quarters was sounded, and USS *Texas* transited the channels swept through German minefields and headed for the beaches of Normandy. (These channels had been cleared by minesweepers of the U.S. and Royal Navies only recently, to avoid giving the Germans advanced warning of the force.) HMS *Glasgow* took the lead and acted as guide for USS *Texas* and the warships in company, with additional minesweepers in advance.

USS *Texas* had to pass through a long line of landing craft while staying in the swept channels, and this caused many anxious moments for the landing craft as the battleship loomed over them out of the dark. There was only one minor collision, with a landing craft that was unable to counter the strong crosscurrents; *Texas* gently nudged her back on course. For the latter part of the approach to the assault area the ship used radar to locate and identify prominent landmarks to fix its precise location. The shoreline stood out on the radar screen as presented in the navigation charts.

On reaching her designated bombardment position at 3:00 a.m. on the 6th, *Texas* was ready to open fire. Crew members above deck watched the prelanding air bombardment, which commenced with pathfinder aircraft dropping clusters of red and green flares over Pointe du Hoc and Omaha Beach. They were followed by 480 B-24s of the Eighth Air Force. Unfortunately, the bombers held off releasing their bomb loads for a few seconds to ensure they did not hit their own troops; as was soon learned, the bombs struck three miles inland and not on the defenses of Omaha Beach.

Omaha Beach had been selected for the U.S. forces; Gold, Juno, and Sword Beaches to the east for the British and Canadians; and Utah Beach to the west for the Americans as well. Omaha Beach was over four miles in length with high cliffs at each end, bristling with defenses, part of the Germans' "Atlantic Wall." The defenses along Omaha Beach comprised 8 concrete bunkers, 35 pillboxes, 6 mortar pits, 35 rocket launchers, and 85 machine-gun nests.

At 5:30 a.m. on 6 June USS *Texas* swung to the west until her port side faced the beach, seven miles away.

The intention was that USS *Texas* would maintain her position heading into the strong current during the bombardment by using her engines, rather than anchors.

At 5:40 a.m. Captain Baker gave the order to sound "Commence firing," and the bugle call was heard throughout the ship over the intercom. The gunnery officer in the armored conning tower ordered, "Commence firing." The ten 14-inch guns of USS *Texas* fired over the heads of the soldiers nearing the beach at a German battery on top of Pointe du Hoc.

Pointe du Hoc was a prominent cliff-top plateau overlooking both Omaha and Utah Beaches. The Germans had constructed gun emplacements for six 6-inch guns, each with a range of ten miles, and an armored observation bunker to direct their fire. With its commanding position over two critical beaches and its strong armament, Pointe du Hoc had been designated as Army "target 1." Pointe du Hoc had already been bombed in the previous months both by the USAAF and the RAF, and unknown to the D-Day planners, the six guns had been moved inland to an emplacement near the village of Grandcamp-Maisy and replaced with deceptive camouflaged tree trunks. The new "Maisy" emplacement still gave the battery commanding coverage of both beaches.

USS *Texas* fired 255 14-inch shells at Pointe du Hoc from 5:50 to 6:24 a.m., averaging 7.5 shells every minute for 34 minutes. Fire was stopped just before the time, 6:30 a.m., when the troops were scheduled to land on the beach from their Higgins landing craft.

The U.S. Army's 1st Division, the "Big Red One," under Major General Ralph Huebner, had been selected to land on Omaha Beach, because of its combat experience in North Africa and Sicily. The soldiers of the Big Red One needed all that experience to survive the German defenses, which turned the beach at Omaha into a killing zone. The Germans had sited their guns to be able to fire along the beach rather than just to seaward. This created crossing fields of fire through which the troops of Big Red One had to advance. Also, the defensive positions were not readily visible to Allied ships and troops.

The initial landing was a bloodbath for the troops, whose plight was made even more desperate by the failure of supporting tanks and artillery to land at the eastern end of the beach at the allocated time, except for five duplex-drive, "swimming" tanks. Twenty-nine

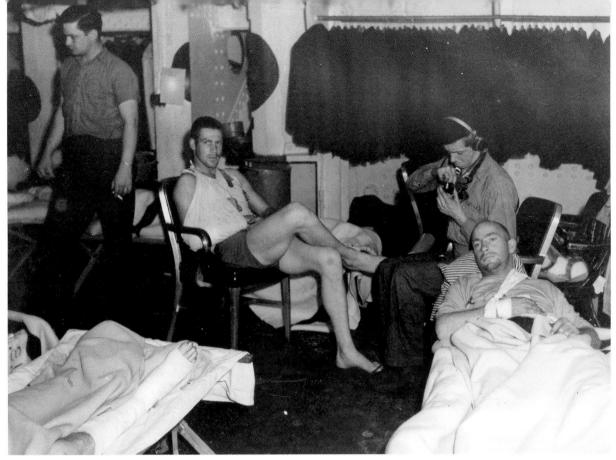

Wounded Rangers from Normandy in a battle dressing station on board USS *Texas*. (NARA)

duplex-drive tanks had been launched from their landing craft but too far from the shore and in rough water; 21 tanks sank with their crews and 3 tanks were inoperative. The troops who survived were stuck on the beach, trying to find protection behind a seawall from German gunfire. To this turmoil was added the next wave of Higgins landing craft with more troops.

Besides USS *Texas* and the other battleships and cruisers of the bombardment force, 12 destroyers were stationed inshore of the heavy ships to provide close supporting fire as needed. The plan was for these destroyers to be between 5,000 and 7,000 yards offshore; however, once they saw the precarious situation of the landed troops, the destroyers moved in to between 800 and 1,000 yards from the shoreline, in several instances touching the sea floor, to give their 5-inch guns greater effect.

Three companies of Rangers from the U.S. Army's 2nd Ranger Battalion had been set to land at the base of Pointe du Hoc, climb the cliffs, and ensure the destruction of the gun battery. Their landing was significantly delayed by poor visibility and a rough sea; worse, a strong cross-current pushed the landing craft to the west. Once they had identified where

they were, their coxswains had to return eastward underneath the cliffs of Pointe du Hoc. By the time they landed, after a delay of 30+ minutes, the naval bombardment had stopped; German soldiers emerged from their bunkers, returned to their defensive cliff-top positions, and used mortars, machine guns, hand grenades, and rifle fire against the Rangers climbing the cliffs.

The sailors on USS *Texas* who were in the open could only watch the near-suicidal climb. Against all odds, the steadfast Rangers reached the top of the cliff, where they found they could use the many craters caused by the earlier 14-inch shells from USS *Texas* as cover. The Rangers soon defeated the remaining German troops, reached the battery, and saw that the guns had been replaced by tree trunks. The Rangers, true to their mission, followed the tracks by which ammunition had been supplied to the guns' new location and destroyed them.

While the Rangers were climbing and the Army troops were landing on Omaha Beach, Spitfires flown by *Texas* pilots and other pilots of VCS-7 were overhead, searching for targets and spotting the battleship's fire to destroy them.

In addition, the ship's own foretop spotting position perceived that the troops on Omaha were unable to advance off the beach, because the roads and tracks leading inland through ravines had been heavily fortified and were being defended. The battleship moved closer to the beach, and at 3,000 yards the foretop was able to locate clearly the location of enemy positions on what the invasion maps referred to as "Exit D-1." The 5-inch guns of the secondary battery then forcibly removed pillboxes, mortars, and machine-gun posts, as well as individual snipers holing up in houses. In essence, USS *Texas* out-sniped the snipers and their rifles with 5-inch guns and explosive shells.

The debris from the fighting, the collapse of the seawall, and destroyed houses made a barrier at the beach end of D-1, which USS *Texas* cleared with accurate fire from her 14-inch guns. With the removal of enemy forces, Army engineers were able to use their bulldozers to create a new ramp from the beach leading inland, which allowed troops to move forward.

The table (next page), based on the ship's after-action report, gives the bombardment action by USS *Texas* that day.

The Spitfires overhead could stay on station as spotters for approximately 45 minutes. It took one hour to fly from Lee-on-Solent, in Hampshire, across the English Channel, locate USS *Texas*, and commence looking for targets. The Spitfires carried an external 35-gallon belly tank for extended range. Each spotting aircraft was accompanied by another Spitfire, the "weaver," whose role was to protect the spotting Spitfire from enemy aircraft. The ideal height for the Spitfires to locate targets was 6,000 feet, well below the altitudes at which enemy aircraft patrolled. Therefore, a spotting Spitfire, whose pilot's attention was necessarily downward, was extremely vulnerable to diving enemy aircraft, unless the weaver intercepted them.

The spotter and weaver Spitfires flew throughout D-Day identifying a number of targets, including troop movements, ammunition dumps, and vehicles, which USS *Texas* destroyed with its powerful guns. Furthermore, the pilots' running radio commentary was appreciated by the officers and crew on the battleship, and sometimes amusing: the effect of the ship's gunfire on targets and the fun of strafing targets of opportunity.

On D-Day USS *Texas* fired 253 5-inch and 445 14-inch shells—the most 14-inch shells fired by USS *Texas* in one day. Spotting Spitfires confirmed accuracy of the ship's gunfire. USS *Texas* recorded no damage from enemy action. (The shock of the ship's gunfire did break a number of cathode ray tubes in the radar equipment and damaged the Huff-Duff antenna.)

German prisoners of war on board USS *Texas*, June 1944. (Texas Parks & Wildlife Department)

Time	Target	Type and Rounds Fired	Type of Spotting	Remarks
05:50–06:24	6 x 155-mm guns. Pointe du Hoc	155 x 14-in AP 100 x 14-in HC	Aircraft	Area neutralized. Hits on casements and emplacements
05:50–06:23	Multiple pillbox, tanks, and MGs	91 x 5-in HC 99 x 5-in COM	Foretop	No enemy action observed after bombardment
06:26–06:30	Fortified position	17 x 14-in HC	Aircraft	Fire effective
07:42–07:47	Strong point, MGs and pillbox	13 x 14-in AP	Aircraft	Direct hits reported by air spot
08:10–08:24	Fortified position with 4x155-mm mortars	26 x 14-in AP	Aircraft	Several direct hits on emplacement reported by plane
10:33–10:56	Mobile field battery	40 x 14-in HC	Aircraft	Fire effective
11:17–11:28	Gun position in wooded area	26 x 14-in HC	Aircraft	Gun silenced
12:23–13:30	Exit D-1, enemy mortar battery behind wall and hedge	6 x 14-in HC	Foretop	Battery neutralized, personnel scattered
12:25–12:26	Pillboxes and snipers in house, Exit D-1	9 x 5-in HC	Foretop	Hits in enemy held area
12:31–12:35	Exit D-1, mortar firing and snipers in house	7 x 5-in HC	Foretop	Direct hits on house. Enemy guns silenced
14:00–14:40	Troop transports, flak station, powerhouse and ammunition dump	18 x 14-in HC	Aircraft	Transports disorganized, 2 guns destroyed, direct hits on ammunition dump and power house
18:15–18:20	Exit D-1, Church steeple used as observation post for mortar fire	9 x 5-in HC	Foretop	Fire effective, direct hits on church steeple
18:57–19:02	Enemy mortar, and snipers	24 x 5-in HC	Foretop	Direct hits on house and wall concealing snipers
19:22–19:25	Small troop concentration and mortar fire	15 x 5-in HC	Foretop	Direct hits on house
19:41–20:11	Troops at crossroads	25 x 14-in HC	Aircraft	Troops dispersed
20:45–21:09	Enemy vehicles	18 x 14-in HC	Aircraft	Fire effective, several hits

AP = ARMOR-PIERCING (PROJECTILE); COM = COMMON (PROJECTILE); HC = HIGH-CAPACITY (PROJECTILE); MG = MACHINE GUN

When night fell USS *Texas* darkened ship and prepared for night bombing raids. Captain Baker gave orders that the antiaircraft guns were not to fire, as non-radar-controlled gunnery was inaccurate and would give away the ship's position. The radio-countermeasure team detected a number of German radio-guided missiles approaching the ship and jammed their receivers so that they fell into the sea close by.

In the early morning of 7 June USS *Texas* was advised that the Rangers at Pointe du Hoc required immediate assistance for their wounded, plus arms, ammunition, and food. Captain Baker was able on his own authority to obtain two landing craft, which he had come alongside to be loaded with ammunition, food, and water. The craft were then directed to land at the foot of the Pointe du Hoc cliffs and unload. The two landing craft returned with 41 wounded Rangers, the body of a Coast Guard sailor (a boat coxswain), and 27 prisoners of war. The ship's surgeons and corpsmen treated the wounded in the sick bay and in temporary treatment spaces. Crew members gave up their bunks to wounded soldiers until they were transferred the following day to a transport ship to be taken back to England for hospital care.

Texas recommenced her bombardment—this time of troops, vehicles, and strongpoints near the French village of Formigny—at 8:04 a.m. on 7 June. Spitfires identified this concentration, and USS *Texas* responded with 35 14-inch shells. At 9:15 a.m. the airborne spotters called for fire on the village of Trévières, where German troops and a strongpoint were located. This target was attacked with eight armor-piercing and 50 high-explosive 14-inch shells; the spotters radioed back that the town was "laid to waste, with many fires." The German troops were killed with survivors displaced. Later, in the early evening, Spitfire spotters located a vehicle column and troops; *Texas* dispersed both, with 26 high-explosive 14-inch shells.

On the 9th USS *Texas* returned to Plymouth to replenish ammunition, fuel, and supplies and to repair the equipment that had been damaged by the shock of her own gunfire. USS *Texas* returned to the Omaha Beach bombardment area on 11 June and provided gunfire as needed. On the 15th, troops of the First U.S. Army located a large concentration of German troops between the towns of Isigny and Carentan and requested gunfire support from USS *Texas*. The range was greater than her 14-inch guns could reach at their maximum elevation of 15 degrees; they needed two more degrees. Captain Baker ordered the flooding of the starboard antitorpedo blisters; the resultant heel of the ship to starboard gave the guns, firing to port, the required elevation and thus range. Relying on the Spitfire spotters, USS *Texas* fired 24 14-inch shells, which caught the German troops out in the open between the two towns, with significant effect. The First Army moved forward and was soon beyond the range that USS *Texas* guns could reach.

It is important to note that on D-Day the strong defense by the German army, coupled with the effect of the bad weather and sea conditions, delayed the movement off the beach and inland. This danger was magnified by the lack of artillery and tanks ashore. Into this catastrophic void USS *Texas* and her accompanying bombardment ships and destroyers delivered crucial—in fact, war-winning—gunfire support that, breaking up the German forces that had kept the Big Red One on the beach. The pilots of VCS-7, wheeling and zooming overhead dodging antiaircraft flak and German fighters, supplied critical intelligence to the ship's gun directors, as did the ship's own spotters in the foretop.

The crew of USS *Texas* undertook on the morning of 7 June the horrendous task of pulling out of the water as many bodies of American soldiers they could before they drifted out to sea and disappeared. These were soldiers who had been killed in landing craft sunk approaching the beach or as they attempted to wade ashore.

On 18 June USS *Texas* left the bombardment area, joined USS *Arkansas* and *Nevada*, and returned again to Plymouth for replenishment. On the 21st they left for Portland on the English south coast, where the U.S. naval advanced amphibious headquarters was, to prepare for the scheduled attack on the French port of Cherbourg. This stop at Portland provided sufficient time for liberty call for the crew.

CHERBOURG

Cherbourg was a key objective. The port would enable the Allied armies to land the large quantities of ammunition, fuel, and food necessary for the advance across France and into Germany. Omaha and Gold Beaches had been equipped with temporary floating "Mulberry" harbors to supply the immediate needs of the armies. The Mulberry at Omaha was destroyed by a powerful storm on 19 June; but the Mulberry at Gold

Beach, while sustaining damage, continued to operate. The Mulberry harbors, in the ten months of operation, handled the arrival of a million tons of supplies, a hundred thousand vehicles, and two and a half million fresh troops, as well as the evacuation of thousands of wounded.

On 25 June USS *Texas* left Portland with *Arkansas* and the destroyers *Barton*, *O'Brien*, and *Laffey* and sailed to Cherbourg to support the 4th U.S. Infantry Division, which had the mission of capturing the port.

At approximately 9:00 a.m. minesweepers started their dangerous work, and at 9:15 a.m. General Quarters was sounded on board USS *Texas* as she moved to her bombardment position. *Texas* was to respond to requests from Army fire-control parties ashore for gunfire on targets they had identified and located, as well as to counter the 20 German coastal batteries. These batteries opened fire on the ship at 12:30 p.m. Relying on Spitfire spotters overhead, USS *Texas* and her supporting ships returned fire. For the next several hours *Texas* was involved in a furious duel with the

The German shell that failed to explode when it hit USS *Texas*. Captain Baker is on the left. (Texas Parks & Wildlife Department)

batteries. Though she continually maneuvered to throw off the accuracy of the German gunfire, the battleship was bracketed by and drenched by the splashes of near misses. The destroyers were ordered to lay a smoke screen to hide both USS *Texas* and *Arkansas* from the German gunners. This created a further problem, as the two battleships maneuvered within close proximity of each other; they once nearly collided, but thanks to radar and quick helm responses disaster was averted.

At 1:16 p.m. a German nine-inch (240 mm) shell hit the top of the armored conning tower, destroying the gunnery periscopes that protruded through it. The shell was deflected by the tower roof's four-inch-thick armor plate and struck the supporting column of the navigation bridge, where it exploded. The explosion vented upward and destroyed the forward section of the bridge, killing the helmsman and wounding other personnel. Fortunately, Captain Baker was outside the pilothouse on the starboard wing; he ordered the evacuation of the bridge and transferred steering control to the conning tower secondary helm position. USS *Texas* maintained her fire while corpsmen and stretcher bearers transferred the dead and wounded sailors to the sick bay along decks drenched by more near-misses. Inside the conning tower, the internal section of the main-battery director periscope sheared off by the shell hit fell and hit Lieutenant Commander Richard Derickson on the head, requiring that he be taken to sick bay.

Eventually, with the aid of the Spitfire spotters of VCS-7 and the other bombardment ships, USS *Texas* destroyed the coastal batteries, but not before she had experienced sixty-five "straddles" and near misses.

Two other issues resulted from this action. A German shell the same size as the one that hit the conning tower ricocheted from the sea surface and hit the port side of *Texas* at frame 19, approximately 12 feet down from the main deck. This shell hit the ship sideways-on rather than point-first and did not explode, but it left a good-sized hole. The damage control party secured the shell, which was found in a warrant officer's stateroom, from moving around by stuffing mattresses around it. The shell would have to wait to be disarmed until the battleship returned to port.

The second issue was on deck at the stern, where there were two quad 40-mm gun tubs manned by the ship's Marine Detachment. At one stage blast and fireballs from the two 14-inch guns ignited the canvas

German shell that failed to explode, Portland Harbor. (NARA)

Hole left by German shell. (NARA)

Shell splashes off Cherbourg, from USS *Texas*. (NARA)

covers that protected the ready ammunition boxes in brackets bolted to the inside of the gun tub. The blast also opened these boxes and spread 40-mm rounds over the hot deck. Concerned that the burning canvas covers might ignite the propellant in the shells, causing them to fire and ricochet around the ship, Sgt. Maj. Vikko Liila, U.S. Marine Corps, responsible for the guns, ordered his fellow Marines to throw the stored shells overboard. This required careful timing, as the men had to move only between their ship's salvos; Marines caught in the open would be seriously injured by concussion. The Marines successfully removed the vulnerable 40-mm shells.

Texas reached Portland on 27 June. During the voyage, the ship's bomb-disposal officer examined the shell and its base, where the fuse was located, but was unfamiliar with the fuse itself, for which there was no documentation on board. Captain Baker advised the harbormaster at Portland that he required a bomb-disposal officer to come out to deal with it. A Lieutenant Sturdevant boarded the ship when it anchored and examined the shell. Lieutenant Sturdevant was unfamiliar with the fuse type but recognized that the shell had to be removed from the ship. So, the two officers rigged a sling, collected a working party, and gingerly moved the shell out of the cabin and along a passageway until it was underneath a hatch to the main deck. The shell was hoisted up to the deck and then passed to a landing craft alongside. Lieutenant Sturdevant, in the landing craft with Ford, initially planned to take the shell out of the harbor to deep water and drop it overboard. However, as they motored across the harbor he noted that the fuse had loosened in its setting and could be removed. He did so, and as the shell was now less dangerous, the two lieutenants decided to return to the ship, where the machine shop could make an impression of the shell's base. From this impression a spanner wrench was cast that was then used to remove the base to gain access to the explosive charge within. Lieutenant Sturdevant then took the shell ashore to his office and work area and steamed the explosive out. He also examined the fuse, determining that the striker had hit the primer but that the primer had failed to ignite the explosive charge.

USS *Texas* was now able to leave Portland and steam to Plymouth and the Devonport Dockyard for repairs to her bridge. When this work was completed on 3 July she moved to buoy D in Plymouth Harbor, and on the 4th back to Belfast Lough for fuel, ammunition, and stores. The catapult was reinstalled on turret three, her Kingfisher aircraft were reembarked, and the pilots returned from flying Spitfires. VCS-7 had been disbanded on 25 June and entered the history books as the shortest-lived squadron to date. During its short existence, 20 combat days, VCS-7 flew 209 sorties over the D-Day beaches and Cherbourg, with one pilot fatality.

THE SOUTH OF FRANCE

On 15 July USS *Texas* sailed from Belfast Lough as flagship of TG 120.8: the aircraft carriers HMS *Emperor*, *Khedive*, *Searcher*, and *Pursuer*, plus the auxiliary anti-aircraft cruiser HMS *Ulster Queen*. The task group was headed for Taranto in the Mediterranean. After passing through the Straits of Gibraltar, the ships anchored in the Mers-el-Kébir Harbor, west of Oran. It had been there that in July 1940 the Royal Navy had neutralized the French fleet at anchor.

USS *Texas* sailed for the "heel" of Italy on 27 July and reached Taranto on the 30th. (Taranto had already played a major, if inadvertent, role in the war.) On the night of 11 November 1940, 21 Fleet Air Arm Swordfish from HMS *Illustrious* had attacked the Italian battleships *Littorio*, *Duilio*, and *Cavour* at anchor, hitting all three. Although damaged, *Littorio* had been able to sail to Naples, the other two battleships having sunk and resting on the harbor floor with their main decks awash. The torpedoes used by the Swordfish aircraft had been adapted to run shallow and not strike the harbor seabed. A U.S. Navy observer on board *Illustrious* sent home a detailed report on the raid. The Japanese navy too was interested in how major ships had been successfully attacked in shallow water: it sent groups of officers to Rome and Taranto, respectively to discuss the raid with the Italian navy high command and to view Taranto Harbor. The raid on Pearl Harbor occurred less than a year later.

Texas used the ten-day stay in Taranto to brief the crew fully on their role in the upcoming invasion of southern France, code-named Operation Anvil. In addition, the United Services Organization put on a show on the forecastle with entertainers from the United States, a morale boost for officers and men.

The purposes of Anvil were to draw German troops away from northern France; land troops, armament, and supplies through the ports of Marseilles and Toulon; and gain access to the Rhone Valley and its communication links to the north. All of this would enable the U.S. Army to move rapidly through France from the south and join the Allied armies breaking out of Normandy.

Texas sailed from Taranto on 11 August with USS *Nevada*, *Philadelphia*, and the French cruisers *Montcalm*

and *George Leygues*. On the 14th, off the west coast of Corsica, the ships joined convoy SF-1A. The convoy comprised ten ships in two columns of five. USS *Texas* took station 2,000 yards astern of the convoy, which proceeded at 11 knots. By 5:00 a.m. on 15 August the battleship was on station off the invasion beach; USAAF bombers flew passed overhead to drop their bombs on their targets before the troops landed.

The invasion of southern France was made on the beaches around St. Tropez by VI Corps, with the 3rd, 36th, and 45th Infantry Divisions. USS *Texas* was allocated target "P-39," a battery of five 8-inch guns protected by rock casements. The Kingfisher was catapulted to begin spotting the ship's gunfire, but neither the pilot and observer in the Kingfisher nor the spotters in the foretop could see the target, because of low-lying clouds and the distance of the ship from the target. The German battery opened fire at 6:50 a.m., and shell splashes were seen ahead of USS *Texas*, which then attempted to locate the target by radar, opening fire at 6:51 a.m. with a two-gun salvo from number-one turret. However, the Kingfisher was unable to spot the fall of shot. A two-gun salvo from turret two was fired, but again the fall of shot was unobserved. Admiral Bryant, on board USS *Texas*, ordered a destroyer, USS *Fitch*, to close the beach and see if she could direct the fire. *Fitch* signaled that the aiming shots had been accurate, and the battleship fired a full ten-gun salvo.

At 7:50 a.m., the cable in the right upper projectile hoist of number-five turret pulled out of its securing clips. The shell car, carrying an armor-piercing round, dropped three decks to the upper handling room, where buffer stocks absorbed the impact without damage. The projectile hoist was repaired by 9:45 a.m.

USS *Texas* continued to fire at target P-39 until just after 8:00 a.m. The American invasion troops landed at 8:00 a.m. and quickly overran the German forces, negating the need for additional gunfire. P-39 did not fire after USS *Texas*' first salvo; when the gun battery was overrun and captured by soldiers of the 3rd Infantry Division, the accuracy and effectiveness of the ship's bombardment was clear.

With the invasion a success, USS *Texas* retired to Palermo in Sicily and then, with *Arkansas*, sailed to Algeria to meet USS *Nevada*. The three battleships, which constituted Battleship Division 5, were ordered on 4 September to return to the United States. Battleship Division 5 entered New York Harbor on 14 September;

USS *Texas* entered the Brooklyn (that is, New York) Navy Yard for dry-docking and repairs. The ship's ten 14-inch guns, which had exceeded their service lives by firing more than 200 shells, were relined. One of the barrels was loaded onto a truck and paraded through Manhattan along Broadway as part of a war-bond drive.

USS *Texas* also received new crew members. These new arrivals and systems needed to be trained and exercised to become an effective team. Once the work was complete the ship was ready to sail to its next arena, which was the Pacific and the war against Japan.

USS *Texas* off the Maine coast, November 1944, in camouflage measure 31A, design 8B. (NARA)

USS *Texas* in camouflage measure 31A, Design 8B in this painting by the artist Carl G. Evers. (U.S. Navy)

WAR AGAINST JAPAN

USS *Texas* off Iwo Jima, February 1945. (NARA)

USS *Texas* arrived at Pearl Harbor on 9 December 1944. Though still far from the war zone, she continued her gunnery exercises, particularly antiaircraft. In addition, the crew painted the ship with Measure 21 camouflage colors of dark blue, to help the ship blend into the color of the Pacific Ocean.

The ship and crew spent Christmas in Hawaii and sailed for Ulithi Lagoon on 9 January 1945. Ulithi is a vast coral-ringed lagoon in the Caroline Islands. The lagoon is 3,750 nautical miles from Pearl Harbor, and *Texas* arrived on the 23rd after a journey of 14 days at ten knots. These numbers fully evoke the vastness of the Pacific and the problems of waging a naval war on this ocean.

The logistical challenges for a task force battling its way westward from Pearl Harbor included battle-damage repair, resupply of fuel, carrier aircraft, ammunition, food, and servicing equipment, ship and equipment upkeep, personnel arrivals and transfers, and the health and morale needs of the men. It should be noted that the Newport Naval War College had war-gamed these logistical scenarios in a "Blue–Orange" (i.e., United States versus Japan) series of games in the 1928–29 academic year. The players, officers of the college's senior class, concentrated on those aspects, as well as on strategic and tactical issues, of a Blue advance westward across the Pacific. The games made clear that advanced bases would be needed.

Service Squadron 10, comprising a variety of repair- and supply-related ships and craft, was ordered to Ulithi Lagoon on 4 October 1944 to establish there a serviceable "floating naval station." Within a month of arrival Service Squadron 10 was able to service a complete task force with its attendant supply ships. Warships could call on a vast organization, with 6,000 shipfitters, artificers, welders, carpenters, and electricians. One of the squadron's ships, USS *Abatan*, distilled water and baked fresh bread and pies. There was a barge that could make 500 gallons of ice cream per shift, and a dry-dock that could lift a 45,000-ton *Iowa*-class battleship. Service facilities could repair, or usually even make, any part a warship needed. Ulithi became the terminus for merchant tankers that supplied the 27 fleet oilers with fuel oil, aviation gas, and diesel oil. Fully loaded fleet oilers proceeded to designated locations at sea, available for underway replenishment. In short, Ulithi Lagoon became a major floating naval base for the U.S. Pacific Fleet.

For the men, there was Mog Mog Island at the northern end of the lagoon for swimming, ball sports, lounging on a Pacific Ocean beach in a tropical setting, and ice cream. The men were rationed to two beers or two colas a day on Mog Mog. For USS *Texas*, Flotta Island of 1918—a freezing, windswept, barren, and sodden place between the cold North Sea and gale-stricken North Atlantic where only two cups of warm tea and possibly a limp, tasteless sandwich from a Royal Navy canteen were available—was a lifetime and two oceans away.

IWO JIMA

The next target was Iwo Jima, an island with three airfields from which Japanese fighters intercepted B-29 bombers on their way to and from Japan. This threat needed to be removed and the airfields used as a stopping point for damaged B-29s returning from their missions. Before Iwo Jima was invaded, USS *Texas* took part in a dress rehearsal around the island of Tinian, which had already been captured, involving exercises with other task force ships over two days. These exercises completed, *Texas* proceeded to Iwo Jima on 14 February 1945, as part of Task Force 54, arriving on the morning of the 16th. The Kingfisher was launched and by 8:00 a.m. was passing back to the ship coordinates of targets for *Texas* to bombard with its 14-inch main armament. However, after five salvos USS *Texas* ceased firing owing to poor visibility, affecting the ability of the Kingfisher to spot the fall of shot. This visibility problem persisted during the day and limited the ship to firing 124 14-inch shells, at artillery emplacements, caves, and troop bunkers. USS *Texas* retired to the nighttime holding area to the northwest of the island until early the next morning.

Captain Baker anticipated air attacks and had the air-defense crews at their action stations by 5:00 a.m. A Kingfisher was launched at first light, and at 7:00 a.m.

USS *Texas* opened fire, first destroying a pillbox and then for one hour on other Japanese positions before ceasing firing. During this lull, a second Kingfisher was launched and the first one recovered. At 9:30 a.m. USS *Texas* resumed firing her main armament and over the course of the morning moved closer to Iwo Jima in support of Navy underwater demolition team swimmers, who were tasked to locate any man-made underwater obstacles in the landing area. Once the swimmers had been recovered a flight of B-24 bombers bombed the beach, in preparation for the return of the swimmers to place explosives on the obstacles located. The swimmers were removed by fast support craft before the explosives were detonated. *Texas* continued with her bombardment of pillboxes, ammunition dumps, and parked aircraft, expending 242 14-inch shells on these targets. The next day, 18 February, was similar, the main armament firing on targets spotted by the Kingfishers.

The next day, the 19th, was D-Day, and USS *Texas* took up her bombardment position off the southwest point of Iwo Jima at a distance of 4,200 yards and commenced firing her 14-inch guns at 6:50 a.m. The weather had cleared, so both the Kingfisher crews and the spotters in the foretop could see the targets they had been assigned, and the ship could now use her 5-inch secondary guns as well. At 8:00 a.m., firing was lifted to allow carrier-based fighters to make two strikes on the landing beaches. The USS *Texas* closed the beaches during these air strikes until she was 2,200 yards offshore. From here she could cover the beach and hinterland with her 14- and 5-inch guns as the Marines approached in their landing craft. It would prove that notwithstanding all the firepower of *Texas*, the other battleships and cruisers, carrier aircraft, and bombers, Japanese defenders survived in caves and bunkers and were quickly able to put up a fierce defense against the advancing Marines.

The battle for Iwo Jima lasted until 16 March, during which time 6,800 Marines were killed. As bloody a battle as Iwo Jima was, one moment became an unforgettable memory for those on USS *Texas* who watched, an image that cemented the reputation of the Marines as national heroes. On 23 February a group from the 28th Marine Regiment fought their way to the summit of Mount Suribachi and raised the Stars and Stripes. This flag raising was captured in a famous photograph and later, for future generations, in

USS *Texas* recovers an OS2U Kingfisher off Iwo Jima, 16 February 1945. (NARA)

a powerful statue: the Marine Corps War Memorial at Arlington National Cemetery in Virginia.

On 4 March a crippled B-29, returning from a bombing mission over Japan, landed at Iwo Jima, on a runway on which Marines and Japanese soldiers were still fighting. By the end of the war 2,251 B-29s had landed at Iwo Jima on their way back from Japan.

USS *Texas* sailed from Iwo Jima on 7 March and returned to Ulithi Lagoon for repairs to and maintenance on her main engines. Also, she took on ammunition, fuel, and supplies. On the 21st she sailed from Ulithi in company with USS *Tennessee* to join the bombardment force for the invasion of Okinawa.

OKINAWA

Okinawa is an island 350 miles south of the Japanese mainland, and from its airfield long-range American fighters and medium bombers would be able to support ground troops invading Japan. To ensure success the Fifth Fleet assembled 40 aircraft carriers, 18 battleships, 200 destroyers, and untold numbers of auxiliary ships and craft, both to battle the defenders and respond quickly to reinforcements coming from Japan.

During the transit to Okinawa, USS *Texas* fueled two destroyers and conducted tactical exercises. At 7:00 a.m. on 25 March the ship was on station in support of minesweepers clearing the approaches to Okinawa. At 2:28 p.m., USS *Texas* opened fire on shore installations; this bombardment lasted until 4:20 p.m., after which the ship sailed to her night retirement position with other members of the bombardment group.

The USS *Texas* repeated for several days this program of support to minesweepers, gunnery off the southern end of Okinawa, and her nighttime position to the east. On 31 March USS *Texas* sailed from her night position to Kerama Retto, or "the Keramas," a small group of islands west of Okinawa. The configuration of these islands, which had been occupied by the Army's 77th Infantry Division on 26 March, offered semienclosed anchorage for refueling and resupply.

On April Fools' Day, 1 April, USS *Texas* took part in a planned deception, a feint landing at Minatago in southeastern Okinawa. At 6:45 a.m. Captain Baker gave the order to commence fire, the 2nd Marine Division landing force boarded their assault craft. The wave of boats steered for the beach, only to turn around

Gun captains' dials and controls. (Judi Burr)

and return to their transports. The purpose was to draw Japanese troops away from intended landing areas on the other side of Okinawa, to the southwest.

The actual landing took place at Hagushi, with the 1st and 6th Marine Divisions and soldiers from the 7th and 96th Infantry Divisions. By the end of the day 60,000 troops were ashore with minimum resistance from the Japanese, whose intention was to fight not on the beach but from strongly defended bunkers and caves. As the Marines and soldiers fought their way to their objectives, USS *Texas* and the other members of the bombardment group steamed around the island responding to requests for naval gunfire and executing their own planned bombardments.

At night on 2 April USS *Texas* joined Task Group 54.2 and retired to the northwest of Okinawa to stand between aircraft coming from Japan and the invasion beaches. On the 6th, three Victory ships carrying ammunition anchored in Kerama Retto to supply the navy. Two of them, *Logan V* and *Hobbs V*, were hit by Japanese "kamikazes," suicide planes, and sunk. The next day, in an action well away from Okinawa, the largest battleship in the world—the Japanese *Yamato*, displacing 72,000 long tons full load and carrying 18-inch guns—was detected heading to support the Japanese army on Okinawa. The *Yamato* was met by 375 aircraft from Fifth Fleet aircraft carriers. These aircraft

attacked *Yamato* and her escorts, sinking *Yamato* with at least ten torpedoes and seven bombs. It is ironic that the process started for the U.S. Navy in 1919, when USS *Texas* launched a Sopwith Camel from a wooden platform built over a turret, and resulted in an armada of aircraft carriers launching waves of aircraft able to sink a battleship two and a half times the displacement of USS *Texas*.

For *Texas*, daily bombardment, nighttime withdrawal, and regular visits to Kerama Retto for replenishment continued until 14 May. Captain Baker kept his crew at General Quarters for 52 days to ensure his ship would be able to respond to kamikaze attack by day or night. Captain Baker explained in his May 1945 action report that "any lesser condition of readiness could not meet adequately the emergencies of suicide bombers. The only answer to an approaching suicide bomber is early and great volume of fire, using every gun that will possibly bear, and early warning by radar cannot always be relied upon." With regard to his men, he stated that they realized the difficulties and "preferred to remain at their stations, resting and sleeping there as opportunity offered, rather than be called up frequently from below." Captain Baker concluded, "The rest period when it finally came, however, was much appreciated."

The USS *Texas* fought off three kamikaze attacks, one of them crashing a hundred feet off her starboard

USS *Texas* aircraft returning to ship, the Pacific 1945. (Texas Parks & Wildlife Department)

quarter. This plane had been fired upon by USS *Arkansas* and *New York* as well; these three battleships, originally built without antiaircraft guns, now put up an antiaircraft gunfire screen for mutual protection.

The seven-week-long battle for the island of Okinawa was bloody even for the Navy, which had to support and supply the Marines and soldiers ashore. The Navy suffered more deaths (4,907) than did either the Army (4,582) or Marines (2,792), predominantly as a result of kamikaze attacks. The Navy lost 32 ships around Okinawa, 26 (including 12 destroyers) to kamikaze attack, and had 164 ships damaged by enemy action.

USS *Texas* fired 2,019 14-inch shells at Okinawa, and 2,643 5-inch. The ship's Kingfisher aircraft flew 60 sorties: 51 for gunfire spotting, 5 patrols, and 4 photographic flights. One of the Kingfishers was hit by enemy antiaircraft fire, which damaged the main float and wounded the rear gunner. The damaged plane capsized soon after landing and sank; both the wounded rear gunner and pilot were saved and returned to the ship.

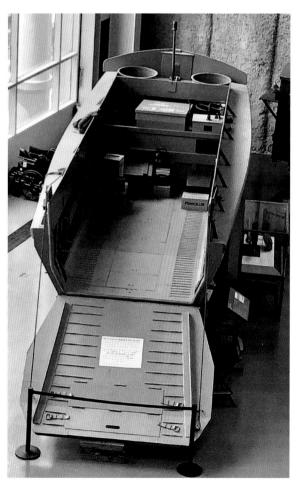

A Higgins boat like those that ferried infantry to beaches on D-Day at Iwo Jima and Okinawa. (Judi Burr)

Notably, USS *Texas* performed all her tasks at Okinawa and at Iwo Jima with no breakdown in her 30-year-old reciprocating engines. Throughout her operational life her engines needed several weeks of routine service and maintenance, as well as overhaul and repairs. Between Iwo Jima and Okinawa operations, however, the ship only had ten days available for maintenance of the main engines, during which time the ship was on four hours' notice and had to get underway for antiaircraft gunnery practice. Additionally, there were many "red alerts," for which USS *Texas* had to sail immediately. The result was over three months of operations with minimal time to effect chronically needed machinery repairs. That her engines stood the strain is a testimony to their designers and builders and to all the engineers who maintained and operated them over the 30 years.

On 14 May USS *Texas* sailed from Okinawa, arriving in Leyte Gulf in the Philippines on the 17th to prepare for the invasion of the Japanese mainland. Captain Baker and Admiral Peter Fischler, commanding Battleship Division 5, were concerned that the antiaircraft battery and its supporting Mark 50 director on board USS *Texas* would not be effective enough for the anticipated aircraft attacks during the invasion of Japan, based on experience off Iwo Jima and Okinawa. Admiral Fischler recommended that one 14-inch-gun turret be removed from USS *Texas* and the weight and space saved be used by installing 5-inch dual-purpose guns and turrets of the type fitted to the *Iowa*-class battleships.

The ship remained in Philippine waters. On 10 August the officers and men were on the forecastle waiting for the evening film to be shown, when the officer of the deck announced over the public-address system that Japan had announced that it would accept the terms of the Allied Potsdam Conference, which called for Japan's unconditional surrender. The war had ended without the need to invade the Japanese mainland. The USS *Texas* and her officers and crew were unaware of the two atomic bombs that had been dropped, on Hiroshima on 6 August and Nagasaki on 9 August, and that the Soviet Union had declared war on Japan on the 8th.

MAGIC CARPET

On 27 August USS *Texas* returned to Okinawa to take part in the Magic Carpet operation that would return American servicemen to the United States. The first men to be taken on board USS *Texas* were released American prisoners of war, who needed the care of sick bay and its doctors and corpsmen. The ship left Okinawa on 23 September, stopped in Pearl Harbor on 4 October for four days, and on the 15th reached San Pedro, where a fleet of ambulances with medics were waiting.

Texas made three more Magic Carpet voyages, between San Pedro and Pearl Harbor. The sailings were: 6 November, Pearl Harbor to San Francisco; 24

Ruthie

San Pedro, Calif.
Pearl Harbor, Hawaii
San Francisco, Calif.
Pearl Harbor, Hawaii
San Diego Calif.
Long Beach, Calif.
Pearl Harbor, Hawaii
San Diego, Calif.
Long Beach, Calif.
Panama City, Panama

Sailor's record of Magic Carpet voyages. (Judi Burr)

November, Pearl Harbor to San Diego, and a nine-day stay in harbor and dry-dock; 15 December, a same-day arrival at and departure from Pearl Harbor for San Diego, where she arrived on 24 December, in time for Christmas.

Then it was time for USS *Texas* to return to her birthplace. She sailed from San Pedro on 21 January 1946, transited the Panama Canal, and arrived at the Norfolk Navy Yard on 13 February. Here, where she had been commissioned on 12 March 1914, she waited to find out what the future had in store. She did not have to wait long. The crew were set to work deactivating her, and once this task was completed the ship was towed to Hawkins Point, near Baltimore, for layup.

USS *TEXAS* TO TEXAS

A permanent home for USS *Texas* where the state of Texas was created, April 1948. (Texas Parks & Wildlife Department)

I n September 1945 the House Naval Affairs Committee listed a number of warships for decommissioning, disposal as targets, or scrapping. USS *Texas* was on this list, owing to her age and need for repairs.

Texas congressmen Lyndon B. Johnson and Albert Thomas began a campaign to save USS *Texas*. They wanted the *Texas* to become a memorial to those who had served on board, specifically during World War II. They convinced the Secretary of the Navy, James Forrestal, to offer the ship to the state of Texas, on the condition that the state agree to maintain her to Navy standards.

Governor Coke Stevenson found that, regrettably, the state government could not accept the offer because of the financial burden, given the postwar economy and the internal infrastructure needs of the state. The governor sent the Navy's offer to the city of Houston, with the assurance that if enough private funds could be raised he would accept the donation of the vessel on behalf of the state.

It was calculated that $225,000 was needed, and a fundraising campaign was commenced by the governor, with the support of Fleet Admiral Chester Nimitz and Secretary Forrestal. However, the fundraising target had not been reached by March 1948, when the Navy advised that the ship was leaving Baltimore for the Houston Ship Channel and that if a berthing slip was not ready for her there, she would be scrapped.

The governor had appointed Lloyd Gregory, vice president and general manager of the *Houston Post*, as chairman of a Battleship *Texas* Commission to take responsibility for the project. Gregory told the readers of the *Houston Post*, "If Texans want their ship they must put up or shut up!" and thanked the donors by printing all their names.

The fundraising target was reached, and on 21 April, the anniversary of the battle of San Jacinto by which Texas had won its independence from Mexico, "Battleship *Texas*," as she can from this point be called, was opened to the public at its new berth. In a ceremony, Charles Baker, who had commanded the USS *Texas* at Normandy and throughout her service in the Pacific, decommissioned the ship, and Assistant Secretary of the Navy Mark Andrews presented her to the state of Texas. In his remarks Admiral Nimitz stated, "By demonstrating the fighting spirit of Texas to our enemies in two world wars this gallant ship has proved worthy of her name. . . . Texans are proud of the privilege of providing a snug harbor for the old 'T,' and preserving her as another symbol of Texas greatness. It is particularly fitting that her final resting place be adjacent to these historic battlegrounds where so much of the Lone Star State tradition was born."

The words "her resting place adjacent to these historic battlegrounds" had prophetic significance: with her officers and crew and navy yards no longer looking after and maintaining her, the waters of the Houston Ship Channel became a deadly enemy, if not as immediately destructive as German shells and Japanese

kamikazes. Over the next forty years the water wore away the steel plates, vents, sea chests, and drainage "overboard" (openings of her hull), so much so that flooding of her double bottom and lower compartments slowly compromised her structural integrity.

"The Spirit of San Jacinto Lives On"

SOUVENIR PROGRAM
Presentation of the
BATTLESHIP U.S.S. TEXAS
TO THE STATE OF TEXAS

SAN JACINTO BATTLEGROUNDS
APRIL 21, 1948

TWENTY-FIVE CENTS
All Proceeds to Battleship Texas Fund

Program for the presentation of USS *Texas* to the state of Texas. (Texas Parks & Wildlife Department)

But Battleship *Texas* continued to add "firsts" to her history. She was the first battleship museum in the United States. Other states followed, taking responsibility for battleships bearing their names: USS *North Carolina*, USS *Alabama*, USS *Massachusetts*, and USS *New Jersey*. In 1966, representatives of these four battleships and of the cruiser USS *Olympia* formed the Historic Naval Ships Association (HNSA), whose purpose is the preserving of the heritage and history of the ships. Since its formation HNSA has grown from five vessels to over 188, including destroyers, submarines, aircraft carriers, plus wooden sailing warships (USS *Constitution*), including foreign ones (HMS *Victory*).

The historical value of Battleship *Texas* was underlined when in 1975 she was designated a National Historic Engineering Landmark, by virtue of her two four-cylinder reciprocating steam engines. In 1977 further recognition was bestowed: Battleship *Texas* became a National Historic Landmark. These two landmark designations reflect official recognition by the U.S. government that Battleship *Texas* is of outstanding historical significance to the country.

It took until September 1983 to bring Battleship *Texas* into a strong governance structure. At that point the Texas Parks and Wildlife Department (TPWD) became the sole authority for the administration, preservation, and maintenance of the battleship. In 1985 a volunteer organization, the First *Texas* Volunteers, offered TPWD their time and services for the upkeep and interpretation of the ship, and the Battleship *Texas* Foundation was created as a separate fundraising entity.

During October 1984 a preliminary preservation plan and program was developed for the ship's restoration and rehabilitation. The plan recognized that the modernization program of 1925–27 had been so comprehensive as to foreclose the possibility of returning the ship to her early configuration, with cage masts and two funnels. The role of USS *Texas* in the Pacific, bristling with antiaircraft guns and able to lay down salvoes of ten 14-inch shells to help the Marines and Army storm Japanese islands, was deemed historically important enough to justify restoration of the ship to that period.

The preservation plan and program laid out the purposes of the development of Battleship *Texas*: to preserve, restore, and reclaim the historical fabric of the battleship; to utilize state-of-the-art methods and materials to facilitate accurate, cost-effective restoration and rehabilitation; and to provide a comprehensive program of interpretation of the battleship and her history. This plan established three levels of priority:

- The preservation of the structural and watertight integrity of the ship.

- Focus on public use and interpretation.

- Provision of a reception area and facilities on the shore.

In accordance with this concept, structure TPWD undertook a major investigation of the structure of Battleship *Texas*; it revealed extensive rust damage to the hull and lower compartments. This investigation concluded that the battleship needed to be dry-docked and repairs to the hull made. Dry-docking was going to be a very costly undertaking, so a new fundraising campaign was launched, with the message 'Save the Battleship *Texas*—She fought for you, now let's fight for her." By October 1986, the Battleship *Texas* Foundation had raised $7,580,000 from military appropriations, a Navy appropriations bill, and private donations.

In order for Battleship *Texas* to be moved from her berth to Todd dry-dock in Galverston, Texas, the channel around the ship had to be dredged. A First *Texas* Volunteer involved, "The biggest task was pumping out [from the ship] 1.5 million gallons of fuel oil and water. The after trim tank, which is below the Steering Room and Steering Gear Room had lost structural integrity and had to be reframed. Welding in the Engine Room was done to restore watertight integrity between the two engine rooms. Replacing gaskets on water-tight doors. Pumps were installed throughout to handing flooding during the tow to Todd's."

The First *Texas* Volunteer further recalled,

On 13 December (a cold morning), at 6AM, tugboats began tying up to the stern and pulled, but the ship did not budge. *Texas* was being held in her berth by 40 years of silt that had washed into the berth and piled up around the hull. Additional tugboats were brought in, till there were six tugs with 25,000 horsepower pulling on the lines and their propeller wash blowing away the silt from the hull. During the pulling, one tug blew an engine and one towline broke with the sound of a high powered hunting rifle firing. By 1:13PM the horse-power pulling on the towlines and propeller wash finally pulled *Texas* from her berth and into the ship channel. By the time *Texas* was turned in the ship channel for the tow south, flooding alarms had already gone off. Because the rudder was frozen 14.5 degrees to starboard, one extra tugboat was needed on the port side at the stern to counteract the rudder. *Texas* arrived at Todd's at 9:05PM. By the time *Texas* was being pushed into

USS *Texas* approaching her new home near the San Jacinto Memorial. (Texas Parks & Wildlife Department)

the Todd's dry-dock, the clearance between the keel and the dry-dock blocks was 6 inches.

For a ship that had sailed through many North Atlantic gales, hunted the German High Seas Fleet in the North Sea, and steamed 728,308 miles under her own power, being towed at 4 knots by multiple tugs for 57 miles along a smooth canal was a new experience.

When Battleship *Texas* was safely on the dry-dock blocks at Todd's Shipyard and the water drained from the dock, her hull leaked water like a sieve. The dockyard workers went to work and kept at it for the next 15 months. The ship was treated from top to bottom. A further 460,000 gallons of water, fuel, and oil were removed, this in addition to the 1,500,000 gallons that had been pumped out prior to the tow. The hull was given an acid bath to neutralize 40 years of immersion in Houston Ship Channel chlorides and then subjected to an abrasive blasting. Around 235,000 pounds of steel forming the outer hull was replaced.

When Battleship Texas reentered the water on 6 August 1989, she was ready to be painted with 9,200 gallons of dark-blue Measure 21, from the top of the fire-control foremast down to the waterline, and to receive a new wooden deck, 26,680 square feet of 16-foot-long four-by-fours of yellow pine.

While all this work was being carried out, the old berth was being upgraded, dredged, and stabilized. Battleship *Texas* was now to float rather than rest on the bottom and be secured with a monopile system as used for offshore oil platforms. This would mean that her underwater hull could be regularly inspected. Battleship *Texas* returned to her upgraded berth at what was now the San Jacinto Battlefield State Park on 28 July 1990.

The interpretation of Battleship *Texas* for visitors and scholars was now resumed and more areas opened so that visitors could see and vicariously experience what it had been like for sailors to live and work on a World War II battleship. Visitors today to the ship can explore from the flag bridge and pilot house, down through several decks to the crew's sleeping quarters, medical rooms, and galley to the boiler and engine rooms. The radio room, plotting room, and central station are open, as is a 14-inch-gun turret, its shell and powder rooms, and the central handling area that hoisted shells and powder to the guns. On the main deck, visitors can turn and elevate 40-mm and 3-inch antiaircraft guns as well as view the size and structure of a 5-inch gun.

An important interpretation undertaking concerning the ship's Pacific campaigns is the restoration of the combat information center to its spring 1945 structure. The role of CIC was to collect, evaluate, and disseminate information received from the ship's radars and radio intercepts. This information was used to control the ship's defensive armament and shore fire, as well as ships and aircraft assigned. CIC was installed on board USS *Texas* in June 1943 and what had been "radar plot." As combat experience revealed an evolving threat environment with decreasing time horizons, radar plot evolved to become a true CIC.

Still, the brackish waters of the mooring basin and the movement of the water caused by the constant passing of large tankers, bulk carriers, and containerships along the Houston Ship Channel to one of the busiest ports in the United States erode the ship's hull and cause leaks. In 2012 and then in 2017 holes of significant size in the stern and on a blister tank caused Battleship *Texas* to list six degrees to starboard. Both times the holes were patched, and the water was pumped out at a rate of 2,000 gallons per minute. An emergency diesel generator and additional pumping equipment was installed in response to these leaks and anticipation of future ones.

TPWD has concluded that Battleship *Texas* needs to be placed permanently in a dry berth. Although studies suggested that her location at the San Jacinto Battleground State Park, near La Porte in the Houston metropolitan area, in a bayou off the Houston Ship Channel, remained the best option, and that the bayou can be sealed off with a cofferdam, which can be drained to provide a dry berth. Battleship *Texas* would need to be moved again to a mooring close by while the dry berth was constructed. Additional studies concluded that internal structural elements needed to be strengthened so the ship could support herself both while floating and in the dry berth.

A prime example of these structural problems concerned the frames that supported the weight of the two engines, at 550 tonnes each, and the engineering work undertaken to overcome it. These frames had been severely damaged and corroded by lengthy immersion in water and were at risk of failing. TPWD had engineers attach six vertical rods to each engine deck, the rods passing through armored decks and attached to the second armor deck. The engines were thereby effectively suspended from the second armor deck by the six rods, relieving the original supporting frames of their weight. This is a further testimony to how well the USS *Texas* had been designed and built. The original purpose of the armor decks had been to protect the ship by keeping armor-piercing shells and bombs from reaching the engines, as well as boilers and magazines. But now the engines hang from the armor decks, protected from the ongoing ravages of the Houston Ship Channel. The next engineering project to be undertaken is to repeat the above exercise for the six boilers in the three fire rooms.

To mitigate the threat of flooding, TPWD has installed new pumps in parts of the ship most at risk. These include the torpedo blisters, the engine rooms, and the vertical trunks that pierce the ship from the weather deck to the lower hull. (These trunks were used to transfer ammunition and equipment down into the ship and were sealed at each deck by armored hatches when not in use.) The vertical trunk aft of gun turret five is the most vulnerable to flooding.

The new pumps needed to be connected to the ship's electrical distribution system for power, and this system in turn had to be upgraded to manage the new load, including new electrical shore-power cabling. A 250-kilowatt self-starting backup diesel generator with a 700-gallon fuel tank has been installed to power the pumps for three days in the event of severe weather isolating Battleship *Texas* from its staff and other assistance.

In 2019, responding to these concerns, state legislature approved a grant of $35 million to fund the needed hull repairs. Additionally, it required TPWD *Texas* to enter a 99-year lease with the Battleship *Texas* Foundation to operate the ship on a stand-alone basis. A substantial amount of work has been undertaken by the nonprofit to prepare Battleship *Texas* to be towed to a dry-dock in the Galveston area, probably in the summer of 2022, and lifted out of the water for repairs to her hull. At this writing she is closed to the public while preparations for the movement are made; to what city in Texas she will return is also "in play" at this writing.

CONCLUSION

USS *Texas*, the first of the U.S. Navy all-big-gun dreadnought battleships, carved out a history for herself and the Navy. USS *Texas* was the first American dreadnought equipped (in 1916) with antiaircraft guns, at the start of a long process to determine how to hit a fast-moving and maneuvering aircraft. Also in 1916, USS *Texas* acted as a test bed for what would become the premier fire-control system in the U.S. Navy. The prototype Ford range keeper installed and trialed on USS *Texas* would be used through World War II and subsequent combat battleship gunfire missions up to the final one, when USS *Wisconsin* firing for the last time 16-inch round at an enemy during Desert Storm in February 1991.

USS *Texas* participated in World War I, sailing through the mine- and U-boat infested North Sea on convoy duty and as a main element of the Grand Fleet of the Royal Navy, searching for the German High Seas Fleet. Finally, when the High Seas Fleet came out to surrender, steaming into the Firth of Forth between columns of the victorious Grand Fleet, USS *Texas* was there, in the middle of the fleet.

The naval air dimension of the Navy, which rose from Eugene Ely's flights in 1910 and 1911, took a major step forward with the launch of a fighter aircraft from USS *Texas*' number-two turret in 1919. USS *Texas* further enhanced the future of naval airpower when as a flagship of the United States Fleet she oversaw two strategic Fleet Problems, IX and X, across the years 1929 and 1930—exercises that pointed to the ultimate demise of the battleship as a frontline asset. Nevertheless, USS *Texas* demonstrated her power as a bombardment platform in support of the Marine Corps and Army during the invasions of North Africa, Normandy on D-Day, and at Cherbourg, the south of France, Iwo Jima, and Okinawa. The reliable firing of her 14-inch and 5-inch guns was a testimony to her builder and to her crew, which stood at General Quarters for 52 days at Okinawa.

USS *Texas*' reciprocating steam engines, holdovers from turn-of-the-century marine design and engineering, remained powerful enough, over 725,000 miles, to carry her through two world wars and four Magic Carpet voyages. The historical significance of these two engines was recognized by the U.S. government by designation as National Historic Engineering Landmarks at the Battleship *Texas* site.

In her day, from commissioning in March 1914 until the commissioning of the aircraft carrier USS *Saratoga* in November 1927, USS *Texas* and her sister dreadnoughts of the U.S. fleet were the largest and most complex pieces of machinery created and operated by man. They were the equivalent of today's manned spacecraft and wide-bodied airliners. In addition, USS *Texas* was a tangible and visible demonstration of U.S. military and diplomatic might, in the same way the nuclear-powered USS *Gerald R. Ford* (CVN-78) is today.

EARLY WARSHIPS NAMED *TEXAS*

A casemate ironclad to be named *Texas* was being built for the Confederate navy at the Richmond Naval Yard. The ironclad was launched but was never completed, as it was captured on 4 April 1864 at the yard by Union forces. Union admiral David Porter appropriated the ship for the Union navy and ordered it towed to the Norfolk Naval Shipyard together with its uninstalled engines, located in a nearby warehouse. In Norfolk the engines were installed, and a trial run was held. However, the ship was sold at auction on 15 October 1867 for scrapping.

The end of the Civil War enabled the United States to concentrate its energies on the development of its economy and the settlement of its vast lands and resources. The U.S. Navy was allowed to atrophy, as the Atlantic and Pacific were seen as sufficiently protective barriers. However, the growing economies of Chile and Brazil enabled the two nations to translate themselves into modern sea powers, by means of the shipbuilding capabilities of Great Britain. The delivery of the protected cruiser *Esmeralda* to Chile and the battleship *Riachuelo* to Brazil in 1883 finally awakened the United States to the threat that such ships posed to American warships, maritime trade, and seaboard cities.

The U.S. Navy held in 1886 a competition for the design of a battleship and an armored cruiser. Both designs had to assume a maximum displacement of 10,000 tons, so as to be coastal-defense rather than oceangoing ships.

The battleship was to become USS *Texas* and the armored cruiser USS *Maine. Texas* was designed by William G. John of the United Kingdom, an established ship designer and draftsman for the Admiralty in London. Once the contract was signed and plans had been received, construction was awarded to the Norfolk Navy Yard in Virginia. Building of USS *Texas* commenced on 1 June 1889 with the laying of the keel. Construction and fitting-out suffered from the difficulties the long shipbuilding hiatus since the Civil War had caused. American iron and steel manufacturers had to develop the technical and managerial capability to cast steel and armor plate to meet Navy requirements. The ship was finally launched on 28 June 28 1892 and commissioned three years later, on 15 August 1895.

Once in commission, USS *Texas* revealed multiple shortcomings in her trials and then her crew and officers encountered multiple shiphandling problems as they learned her new technology. This resulted in the ship earning the nickname "Old Hoodoo."

The sinking of USS *Maine* in Havana Harbor in February 1898 led to the Spanish-American War, and USS *Texas* joined the U.S. fleet off Santiago, Cuba. By now an efficient fighting ship, on 12 June 1898 she entered Guantanamo Bay to support the 1st Battalion of U.S. Marine Corps in occupying the bay. *Texas* supplied the Marines with two Colt machine guns, ammunition, and fresh water from her distillation plant. In addition, she bombarded the Spanish fort on Cayo del Toro at 2:06 p.m., stopping at 3:20 p.m. having destroyed the fort. Returning from Cayo del Toro she came into contact with a Spanish Bustamente mine that fouled one of her propellers but did not explode.

The occupation of Guantanamo Bay was critical to the U.S. Navy, as it provided calm waters in which ships could be coaled and resupplied with stores and ammunition. This base enabled the fleet to remain on station for the blockade of Santiago and of the Spanish fleet at anchor in the bay.

To force the destruction of the Spanish fleet, the U.S. V Army Corps, under General William R. Shafter landed at Daiquiri east of Santiago on 22 June 1898. Subsequent action in this operation included the charge up San Juan Hill by Teddy Roosevelt's "Rough Riders."

On 3 July 1898, the Spanish fleet under the command of Admiral Pascual Cervera sailed from Santiago into the welcoming arms and guns of the U.S. fleet. USS *Texas* opened fire at 4,200 yards on *Maria Teresa* with her port battery but then had to go astern to avoid USS *Brooklyn*, which had cut across her bow. The aft 6-inch gun on board *Texas* registered a hit on the destroyer *Furor* that caused it to sink. While maneuvering USS *Texas* suffered two hits from the 5.5-inch guns of *Oquendo,* but they caused only superficial damage. Back up to speed, the ship joined USS *Brooklyn* and *Oregon* in chasing *Cristobal Colon* westward for approximately 75 miles along the southern coast of Cuba. When USS *Oregon* approached within range of her 13.5-inch guns, *Oquendo* turned from the fight, beached herself and opened her sea cocks to avoid capture. The battle of Santiago was over. *Texas* and the U.S. fleet had secured a major victory over a European naval power.

Following the war and her return to New York, USS *Texas* patrolled the East Coast, but was soon obsolete: the U.S. Navy was rapidly growing and developing a dreadnought fleet. Accordingly, on 15 February 1911 her name was changed to *San Marco* and the *Texas* name assigned to a new battleship, a dreadnought.

USS *TEXAS* (BB-35)
AUTHOR'S ACKNOWLEDGMENTS

The author wishes to acknowledge the significant help and assistance of the following: Andy Smith, Ship Manager, and Sarah Conlon, Curator, Battleship *Texas* State Historic Site; Herb Powers, Battleship *Texas* volunteer; Charles Swift, Managing Director/Supervisory Museum Curator, and Traci Logan, U.S. Naval Academy Museum; Damien Allan, Fleet Manager, Australian National Maritime Museum; Vincent O'Hara, Naval author; Dr. Leona Sparaco, St. Mary's College; Dr. William B. Cogar, Chief Executive, Historic Naval Ships Association; Susan Plas and Denise Myerscough, of East Lake Community Library, and my wife Judith, who researched and assembled the historic photographs and took photographs of Battleship *Texas*.

Bow view of USS *Texas*, the only remaining dreadnought battleship. (Judi Burr)

FROM THE BATTLESHIP
TEXAS FOUNDATION

When Battleship *Texas* opened to the public in April 1948, she was the first United States Navy warship donated to a non-U.S. government entity. Once again, she was leading, but this time she was not leading into harm's way or in technological innovation. She was leading a new generation of remembrance, memorialization, and honoring those who served by becoming not just an old worn-out battleship on display but a shrine to all Texans who served in the World Wars.

In this early era of American museum ships, Battleship *Texas* and the State of Texas sailed in unknown waters. Sure, there were earlier museum ships or ships on display—*Constitution, Oregon, Mikasa,* and *Victory,* to name a few. But none were ever run by a non-naval entity, and that presented a raft of challenges. The first major challenge was new legal mechanisms had to be created for the ship to even be donated by the Navy, and a new Texas government entity had to be created to receive and operate *Texas.* Congress passed Public Law 649 (1946), creating the legal framework to allow and govern all future U.S. Navy ship donations. The Texas legislature would create the Battleship Texas Commission to receive and operate the ship. Following in her wake, Alabama, North Carolina, and other states adopted the commission management model for their namesakes.

Perhaps the most significant challenge that *Texas* met was that no one had ever tried to maintain a capital ship with a crew smaller than an admiral's staff and limited financial resources. Especially an older ship with as many hard sea miles as *Texas* had on her. Over the years, these challenges were met with "innovative" solutions. Solutions like: ballasting her inner bottom tanks with brackish Houston Ship Channel water so the ship could safely ride a hurricane or replacing her severely deteriorated and unsafe original pine deck with concrete. These quick and financially possible solutions unintentionally created long-term threats to the life of this magnificent man of war. The brackish ballast water weakened her bones and wrecked her unique 1925 torpedo blisters; the concrete deck cracked and rainwater entered the ship, accelerating interior deterioration.

Unfortunately, Battleship *Texas* was leading as a cautionary tale. Since 1988, the State of Texas has spent $100 million addressing the deterioration that these solutions and general resource starvation caused to *Texas.* Her road to recovery started with her 1988–89 drydocking and was followed by two rounds of major structural repairs between 2013 and 2018 while floating in her berth and open to the public. Between 2012 and 2018, Battleship *Texas* was beset by a series of catastrophic flooding events, illustrating how much danger the ship was still in despite the 1988 drydocking and following structural repairs.

In 2019, the Texas legislature appropriated $35 million to repair the ship's hull. At the same time, the legislature directed Texas Parks and Wildlife Department (stewards of the ship since 1983) to enter a management agreement with a qualified non-profit to operate *Texas* for the state of Texas. Battleship Texas Foundation took over the ship's operations in August 2020 with a mandate for *Texas* to be operationally self-sufficient. And in August 2022, we successfully and safely got the ship into drydock without the smallest flooding or incident. While in drydock, we are repairing her superstructure and hull, and replacing her always problematic torpedo blisters from the waterline down. In May 2023, the Texas Legislature approved another $25 million to continue repairs to the ship's hull and other critical improvements while she was still on drydock. This additional funding should completely address the 75 years of deferred maintenance in her and breathe long life into this enduring world war warrior.

We firmly believe that the long-term future of the ship is bright. The visibility and increased public engagement that the tow prep, tow, and ship being in drydock has given *Texas* are incredible. During the tow, there was an estimated 2.55 billion media impressions alone. This visibility would not have been possible without the funding, support, and public-private partnership we have with the State of Texas. The public-private partnership allows us to operate the ship with the flexibility of a non-profit, while the State (who owns *Texas*) serves as a safety net for the Battleship *Texas* to ensure her integrity and longevity. The increased public engagement and this partnership are driving the renaissance of *Texas* and opening new ways to tell her story. Our collective vision for the ship is to immerse visitors in the sights, sounds, smells, and touch of being aboard *Texas* in 1945. To deepen the immersion, we are working with partners to develop interactive holograms of sailors, Marines, and their officers to tell their stories and the stories of their ship in their duty stations. And using technology wherever practical to better tell the story of this old WWI battleship that made history in WWII and put that story in the context of US and world history.

It is our desire to make *Texas* engaging to the average 21st-century visitor without sacrificing the authenticity and integrity of the ship. As with every museum ship, museum, or attraction, visitor engagement is critical to the financial success and, thus, the long-term health of Battleship *Texas*. The strength of our partnership with TPWD, *Texas's* renaissance, and the public's heightened interest in the ship will ensure that *Texas* will be healthy and successful and continue to lead well into the future.

Travis Davis
Vice President of Ship Operations
Battleship *Texas* Foundation

(Battleship *Texas* counterclockwise from the top)

Underway in the Houston Ship Channel shortly after departing her former berth at San Jacinto State Historic Site, 31 August 2022. Photo taken from the foremast, looking aft.

In the Galveston Ship Channel, 31 August 2022. Photo taken from the foremast, looking forward.

Being positioned in the dry dock on 31 August 2022. The small dry dock forward of the ship will be brought in and used as a work platform after the ship is out of the water.

In dry dock at Gulf Copper Shipyard, Galveston. Workers have removed several sections of the starboard side torpedo blisters and begun blasting, priming, and installing new steel on the ship's original hull. The port side torpedo blisters are still intact, including the forward port side bilge keel. The scrap metal piled on the dock is from the starboard side torpedo blisters.

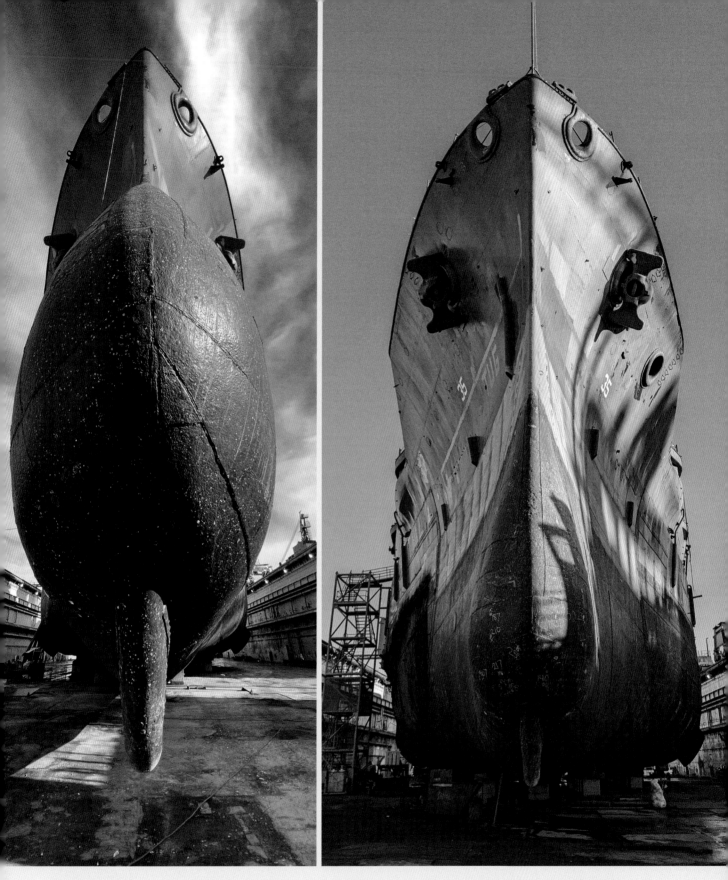

(Left) A close view of Battleship *Texas*'s bulbous bow, as well as the dead-eye under the bow used to attach the chains for paravanes during WWI and WWII.

(Right) A view of the ship's exposed original hull on the starboard side juxtaposed with the intact torpedo blister on the port side.

(Clockwise from the top) Resolve Marine's naval architect, Taylor Reiss, posing at the stern before yard workers removed the 30 years of marine growth. The port side propeller shaft opening (blanked) is visible on the left. The careful reader may observe the remains of the propeller shaft support struts (cut in 1948) between the shaft's opening and the rudder.

The wood base underneath one of Battleship Texas's 5-inch /51 caliber guns (removed for restoration).

Just inside Boiler Room #3, starboard side. The ship's boiler rooms are mostly unrestored.

A close up of severely degraded torpedo blister plating. The weld outline is a section that was replaced in the 1988–1990 dry docking. Just to the right of the weld is a salvage patch applied by divers between 1990 and 2020.

(Clockwise from the top) Gulf Copper workers removing the expanding marine foam installed in the torpedo blisters in 2020. This a rigid, closed-cell foam that sealed existed leaks, mitigated new leaks that might form, and mildly reinforced the structure of the torpedo blisters.

Gulf Copper workers cleaning up chunks of marine foam removed from the ship's aft trim tank.

Inside the aft trim tank looking out.

Several accesses have been cut into the forward starboard side torpedo blisters to remove the marine foam. The foam is flammable, so the accesses were cut with a water jet system. Gulf Copper can then remove the foam with a high-pressure water jet or mechanically.

(From the top) Scrap steel from the starboard torpedo blister. In front of the pile is a flooding valve, used to counterflood a torpedo blister tank in the event water is taken in on the opposite side.

Three of six 5-inch/51-caliber guns removed from Battleship Texas for restoration. The use of a workshop facility in Houston was donated by NRG in support of this project. Temporary supports in place at the stern while hull plating has been removed. Extensive structural repairs were done in this compartment by Taylor Marine in 2013.

Because of concerns about the thickness of the hull in this space, new framing that was installed could not be safely welded to the hull at that time and was instead sistered to original framing. This project will, in effect, complete those repairs done by Taylor Marine.

(Clockwise from the top) A 5-inch/51-mount (center), 3-inch/50-mount (right), and 3-inch/50-caliber gun with a fresh coat of primer.

Gulf Copper workers applying primer to the exposed original hull.

Battleship *Texas* as workers prepare to remove the marine foam from the torpedo blisters.

The first torpedo blister module being installed on the starboard side. Gulf Copper is able to fabricate 8-frame sections (about 32 feet wide) of the torpedo blister on shore, then crane the module into place on the ship. The reconstructed torpedo blisters differ from the originals in two major ways. First they are entirely welded construction, where the original blisters were entirely riveted construction. Second, they extend downwards just to the point where the original blisters began to curve under the ship, then are given a flat bottom at that point. This will make future maintenance easier by eliminating the difficult-to-access spaces at the bottom and providing a flat working platform in the event a tank entry is necessary in the future.

WORLD OF WARSHIPS

World of Warships is a free-to-play naval warfare-themed massively multiplayer online game produced and published by Wargaming. Like their other games, *World of Tanks* (WoT) and *World of Warplanes* (WoWP), players take control of historic vehicles to battle others in player-vs-player or play cooperatively against bots or in a player-vs-environment (PvE) battle mode. *World of Warships* (WoWs) was originally released for on PC in 2015, the PlayStation 4 and Xbox One console versions, titled *World of Warships: Legends*, followed in 2019, and was released on the PlayStation 5 and Xbox Series X/S in April 2021.

Developed by Wargaming d.o.o in Belgrade, Serbia, *World of Warships* (PC) currently has millions of registered players—playing on four main servers across the globe. Over 500 dedicated staff members work on a four-week update cycle to bring new features, ships, and mechanics to the game—keeping game play fresh and inviting to new players. The game features over 650 ships, spread across 12 different in-game nations. Ships are designed based on historical documents and actual blueprints from the first half of the 20th century, and it takes from two to six man-months on average to create each of these ships. There are over 23 ports to choose from, and 16 of them are recreated based on historical harbors and port towns.

There are five different ship classes: destroyers, cruisers, battleships, aircraft carriers, and submarines, with each class offering a different gameplay experience. Ships are arranged in tiers between I and X; players must progress through ship classes and tiers to reach tier X. Ships of tier X represent the pinnacle of naval engineering from World War II and the early

Cold War era. Each warship needs a naval commander to lead it into the battle. There are many commanders to choose from in *World of Warships*, including over 15 iconic historical figures. In *World of Warships* players can battle on more than 40 maps. There are seven different permanent or seasonal Battle Types to choose from: Co-op Battles, Random Battles, Ranked Battles, Clan Battles, Brawls, Scenarios, and Training. From time-to-time additional Event battles are held. Additionally, within Battle Types there are four different Battle Modes available: Standard, Domination, Epicenter, and Arms Race.

Texas made her *World of Warships* PC debut in May of 2016 as an American tier V premium battleship; since then she has become a fan favorite. *Texas* is also available in *World of Warships: Legends* – on console. See *Texas* in person, then take her into battle today in *World of Warships*.

Experience epic naval action in *World of Warships: Legends*—a global multiplayer free-to-play online console game in which you can conquer the seas on the decks of history's greatest warships! Recruit Legendary Commanders, upgrade your vessels, and stake your claim to naval domination alongside and against players from around the world in fast-paced 9vs9 battles. Take control of over 450 destroyers, cruisers, battleships, and aircraft carriers—a range of ships that's perfect for every playstyle, whether it's an all-guns-blazing approach, more careful and methodical attacks, or tactics that are unique to you, with even more possibilities created by the unique Commander system. New content in the form of ships, Campaigns, events, Bureau Projects, and more arrives regularly! Each update brings new features to shake things up in the game, alongside impressive graphics, including full 4K support for next-generation platforms. Develop Legendary vessels such as *Yamato* from the ground up in the Bureau, finish epic Campaigns to gain exclusive patches and powerful new ships, and compete in Ranked Battles Seasons for a ton of rewards!

Wargaming proudly supports various charitable causes that members of the gaming and history community deeply care for.

The rating of the turret captain was established in the U.S. Navy in the early 1900s, in the period of rapid construction of the fleet and emergence of a large number of ships with turret artillery. The functions of the turret captain—who ranked next to the turret commander—was to ensure fail-safe operation of the gun mount, to instruct the turret personnel, and to monitor how servicemen performed their duties.

The turret captain's patch remained nearly unchanged since 1904. It was worn on the right sleeve and was abolished in 1949 together with the rating, becoming merged with the rating of the gunner's mate.

Supporting veterans and servicemembers

- Operation Lifeboat (2020) raised $150,000 USD for Stack Up's mental health awareness helpline
- Remembrance charity drive (2020) raised $45,000 USD for Help for Heroes, who supports UK veterans and service members
- Project Valor (2017) saw WoWs, WoT, and WoWp raising $75,000 USD for a veteran housing program

Preserving historical ship museums

- $50,000 USD raised for the restoration of USS *Batfish*, Muskogee (2019)
- $400,000 USD raised for the restoration of USS *Texas*, Houston (since 2017)
- $20,000 USD raised in partnership with the French-speaking community for the restoration of the submarine *Espadon* (2021)

Supporting local community

- $78,000 USD raised for Team Rubicon and the victims of Hurricane Harvey in 2017
- $106,000 USD raised with WoT and WoT:MA for the Hawai'i Community Foundation Maui's Strong Fund in September 2023

One of the first AA guns of the U.S. Navy, the Mark 10 with a caliber of 76-mm, was developed in 1913–1915 on the basis of an earlier system, the Mark 6, widely used as a secondary battery on the U.S. ships built in the 1900s. The Mark 10 gun could fire at elevation angles of up to 85 degrees. Formally, it had a dual purpose, as it could theoretically attack both air and surface targets. However, the Mark 10 was not sufficiently effective in either. In the first case, because it had only manual aiming, in the second case, because the shells were too light.

Until the late 1920s, 76-mm Mark 10 guns were almost the sole AA artillery systems mounted on large warships of the U.S. Navy. *New York*–class battleships were among the first to receive them during rearmament in 1916.

Mark 10 mounts, two per ship, were already included in the design of Omaha-class light cruisers, which began to enter service in 1923.

The United States Naval Institute (USNI) has been a proud partner of *World of Warships* and Wargaming since December of 2019. Wargaming has a made a commitment to naval history through various programs and events of over the past years. They produce excellent video content with their *Naval Legends* series on YouTube, and host events aboard museum ships where members of the gaming and naval history community can get together and experience the living-history in person. *World of Warships* and Wargaming are also great sponsors of HNSA (Historic Naval Ships Association). USNI thanks Wargaming and *World of Warships* for their continued support of the naval history community and participation in this Naval History Special Edition. Please see the back cover for a special offer for *World of Warships* PC and *World of Warships: Legends*.